# light
## the Window

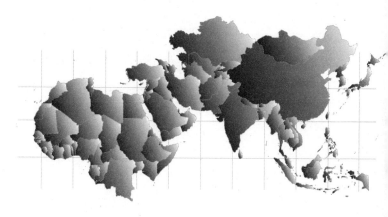

Edited by Floyd McClung

PUBLISHI
A Ministry Of Youth With A
P.O. Box 55787, Seattle, WA

D0377144

YWAM Publishing is the publishing ministry of Youth With A Mission. Youth With A Mission (YWAM) is an international missionary organization of Christians from many denominations dedicated to presenting Jesus Christ to this generation. To this end, YWAM has focused its efforts in three main areas: 1) Training and equipping believers for their part in fulfilling the Great Commission (Matthew 28:19). 2) Personal evangelism. 3) Mercy ministry (medical and relief work).

For a free catalog of books and materials write or call:

YWAM Publishing

P.O. Box 55787, Seattle, WA 98155

(425) 771-1153 or (800) 922-2143

**Light the Window: Praying through the Nations of the 10/40 Window**
Copyright © 1999 by Floyd McClung Jr.

Published by Youth With A Mission Publishing
P.O. Box 55787
Seattle, WA 98155

ISBN 1-57658-150-0

**Printed in the United States of America.**

# Alphabetical Listing of Nations

# Why Pray? Why Go? Why Missions?

*Seven Reasons to "Light the Window" for Jesus*

That part of the world we call the 10/40 Window is covered in spiritual darkness. Hundreds of millions of people are lost without Christ, separated from Him by spiritual darkness and deception. There are reasons, biblical reasons, why it is the will of God for every Christian to be part of "lighting the window" for the Lord Jesus. I have listed seven of those reasons below.

However, these reasons will remain just one more list of things you ought to do someday unless you submit your response to the Lord Jesus right now. May I request that you stop right now and pray? Would you please ask the Lord to speak to your heart as you read through this list? In fact, why don't you dedicate yourself to being available to spread God's glory and share His passions for the church and the nations of the earth. Thank you.

## The Lamb Is Worthy

At the end of time people from every tribe and tongue and people and nation will gather around the throne of God to honor the Lamb of God, all worshipping in their redeemed cultures and music styles. They will gather joyously around the throne of God and celebrate the victory He has won on their behalf.

The One who died a shameful death to redeem the peoples of the earth will be the object of honor and praise for all eternity. All of history will be consummated in the praise of the One who gave Himself for us. He died to make us a kingdom of priests. He set us free from religion and fear and superstition so we might freely enter His throne room of grace. Everything is headed for that day. All we do that has meaning will find its fulfillment at that celebration. May it come quickly, Lord Jesus!

Missions is not about church programs or missionary outreaches, budgets or faith giving, missionaries dressed in strange costumes, or even about the lost people or the needs of hurting masses. It is about Jesus, the Lion who became a Lamb, the Redeemer of all peoples, the Savior of the world! It is for Him! We do missions so He will receive the just reward of His suffering and the praise that is due the One who is the Creator and Redeemer of all things!

### The Spirit Is Moving

We are living in the time of the greatest revival in the history of the church. There have been times in church history when the Spirit has moved on one continent, and then other times when the Spirit has moved on another continent. What is unusual about this period of history is that the Spirit of God is bringing millions of people to Himself, simultaneously, on *every continent.* The church is growing mightily in China, Indonesia, India, Korea, Latin America, Africa—literally all over the world.

God brought down the wall, and the Communist nations of Eastern Europe, and now His Spirit is tearing down walls of fear and cultural separation that hide Muslims and Hindus and Buddhists from the gospel. It is God's gracious invitation and the church's sacred privilege to participate in this unprecedented move of the Holy Spirit. Who would want to miss out on what our Father is doing on the earth? Not me!

God has chosen this time to gather people from all the peoples of the earth in a way He has never done before. Therefore, *it is the will of God for the church to be part of what He is doing.* The *church* is what God is doing; He is raising up a people for Himself from among all the peoples of the earth, so that He might fill the earth with His glory.

### The Lost Are Dying

Most of earth's population will spend eternity separated from God if they do not have a chance to hear the good news of God's salvation. Hell is real, and though many evangelicals believe theoretically in hell, they don't really believe that a "good God will send people to hell."

May God burn into our hearts the terrible reality of man's lostness without a Savior. Men and women need forgiveness of sins. There is no other than the Name of Jesus given among men whereby a person can be saved. It is by hearing, believing, and calling on that Name that people are rescued from a certain, eternal separation from God.

## The Poor Are Suffering

We easily become immune to the horrendous suffering of the victims of drought, famine, poverty, and injustice. It is only by the grace of God that our hardened and calloused hearts can be filled with the compassion of Jesus. The Bible says that when Jesus looked upon the crowds, He had compassion. May we have the same response, whether it is to a neighbor in need, a child's face in a Christian advertisement, or a news broadcast from the Horn of Africa. We know the statistics, we see the faces, now it is time to pray. And to go. And to be Jesus to those without hope.

## The Church Is Commissioned

Jesus commanded us to go, and *go* means a change of location. We have been commissioned to go, teach, baptize, and make disciples. There are people waiting for Christians to obey. Whether it is the village in North Africa that requested a missionary, or tribesmen in the mountains of Tibet, they wait. They wait for our obedience. The issue is not whether or not we are called. All are called. All are commissioned. It is a matter of location. Willing hearts hear His voice. The Lord Jesus said to His disciples, "As the Father sent me, so send I you…"

## The Believers Are Perishing

Without a vision greater than the pleasures of our culture and the comforts of life, we will perish. We must get involved in the nations. It is not enough to send our money, because money does not have to lay down rights, weep, or give of itself. It is not enough to send native workers, because native workers cannot pray, love, and disciple in our place. God uses people to reach people. He uses people to encourage faint hearts. If for no other reason, we must go for our sakes. If not, we will surely perish. For the sake of the church at home, we must give our very best, lest we die from lack of sacrifice, from lack of personal involvement. If we will not, if we believe not, we will perish.

## The Father Is Waiting

The highest motivation for preaching the gospel is not what lost or needy people receive from our efforts, but what God receives from them. Missions is first and foremost about God. He created the nations to seek after Him and find Him (Acts 17:24–26). He brought them into existence so they might find their satisfaction in their Creator. To paraphrase John Piper, God is most glorified when the nations are most satisfied in Him.

Above all things, we must go and we must pray, because the Father is waiting. He longs for the worship and obedience of His creation. He made the nations. He made them for a purpose. Like the father in the parable of the prodigal son, God is yearning for the peoples of the earth to come home to Him, so that the whole earth will be filled with His glory.

Dear Father,

Please fill my heart with the dream that is in your heart, the dream and longing of having a people for yourself made up of people from every tribe and tongue and people and nation.

May your passions become my passions, dear God. Please deliver me from small and petty dreams, dreams of security and fortune and personal ambition. Give me a passion to see You wor-shipped in all the nations of the earth. I want to live for one thing and that is Your Son being worshipped in every place and by every people.

And please use me to make that dream a reality, no matter what it costs.

In Jesus name, amen.

Floyd McClung
YWAM All Nations
Trinidad, Colorado
ywammv@allnations.org

# Introduction

Most of the people in the world who have never heard about Jesus live in a "window" located between 10 degrees and 40 degrees north latitude. If you looked at a world map, this window stretches from North Africa across the map to Japan and includes the Middle East, Central and South Asia, Southeast Asia, China, and the Far East.

Inside the 10/40 Window, as it is called, you will find 95% of all the people in the world who have yet to hear the gospel. Forty-seven percent of the world's total population lives in just two of the countries in the window, India and China. Sixty percent of all the people on the planet live in just five countries in the window: China, India, Bangladesh, Pakistan, and Indonesia.

It is my prayer that the vision of the Lamb of God being worshipped in every place by every people will captivate your heart, if it has not already. Worship is the goal and reason for missions. And when you are gripped by the vision of Jesus being worshipped in languages never before heard in heaven, you will be spoiled for the ordinary!

So read on, and get ready for the Spirit of God to pierce your soul. It happened to me in 1995 when I was gathered with a few students at All Nations Institute to intercede for countries and cities in the 10/40 Window. Unexpectedly, God visited a rather dry, early Saturday morning prayer meeting. Six months later I was visiting one of the countries we prayed for in Central Asia. Now we have workers there and more are preparing to go. Prayer is dangerous!

Every time you pray, the living God listens. And He answers. That is His promise. He said to Jeremiah, "Call unto me, and I will answer you, and will show you great and mighty things you know not"(Jer. 33:3, editor's translation). Jesus told His disciples, "...if two of you on earth agree about anything you ask for, it will be done for you by my Father in heaven. For where two or three come together in my name, there am I with them" (Matt. 18:19–20).

# India

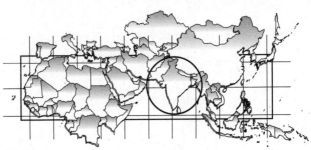

**Capital:** New Delhi
**Population:** 1,042,512,060
**Languages:** Hindi, English, and 16 other official languages
**Major Religions:** Hinduism, Islam, Buddhism, Christianity, Animism
**Major People Groups:** There are almost 2,000 people groups in India!
The largest include Hindi, Marathi, Bengali, Urdu, Bihari, Gujarati,
Banjara—and many more!
**Strategic Town or City:** Mumbai (Bombay)

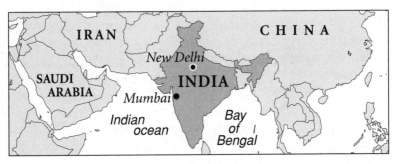

Church history tells us that Thomas, the disciple of Jesus, died in Southern India. Today, 2,000 years later, the church in India is exploding in size. This phenomenal growth includes the northern states of this vast land, which were once considered the graveyard of missionaries.

At the same time, religious persecution is also accelerating. Over 40 incidents of violence against religious minority groups (Christians and Muslims) have been reported in the state of Maharashtra in recent months. The present Indian government is backed by religious nationalists and is committed to turning the secular government of India into a Hindu state.

The largest religious festival in the world, the Kumb Mela, is held in India. Hindus gather by the millions to fast, sacrifice, parade, worship their gods, and invoke the blessings of their deities.

India is an incredible mosaic of cultures and religions. Four of the world's most influential religions were born in India: Hinduism, Jainism, Sikhism, and Buddhism. Hindus make up the largest portion of the population, although India is also home to the world's second largest Muslim population.

Hinduism in India is enforced by Brahmins, the high-caste elite who hold 85% of all government jobs though they only comprise 2% of the population. Over 350 million tribals, untouchables, and other backward castes are growing weary of Brahmin oppression; they are ready to throw off the yoke of bondage, but for what? These millions of disenfranchised people are ready for belief in something that will give them dignity and spiritual liberty.

This is India's hour! She is ripe for the greatest mass movement to Christ in the history of Christianity. One researcher predicts that in the tribal belt of central India alone there will be 4 million Hindu converts to Christ in the next 30 years!

## Prayer Points

- Whenever there is a mass movement to Christ, there is spiritual opposition. Pray for the gates of hell not to prevail against the onslaught of the church of Jesus Christ!
- Pray for the tribal groups of India's poor. Many of them are already coming to Christ, especially the Banjara. Intercede for leaders among them to be raised up, for courage in the face of Brahmin oppression, and for boldness in proclaiming Christ!
- Intercede for the northern states of India, especially Uttar Pradesh and Rajastan. Intercede for village workers, church planters, and indigenous leaders. One Bible school in northern Rajastan reports over 900 churches planted by its students in the last 20 years!
- Ask the Father to keep the doors open for workers from other lands. Indian brothers and sisters deeply appreciate those who

come to labor among them as long they come in humility as servants of the church and the poor.

- There are over 500,000 villages in India without a single Christian! Pray for village workers! The Lord of the Harvest is well able to raise up workers, but we must ask Him to do so. It has been said that 1,000 teams of church planters could each go to a different village in India every week for ten years and the teams would never once bump into each other, so great is the need!

- Pray for a vision amongst the believers of India for cross-cultural missions. India not only needs the world, but the world needs India! The church in India has much to teach us about simplicity, sacrifice, courage, and spirituality.

# Mauritania

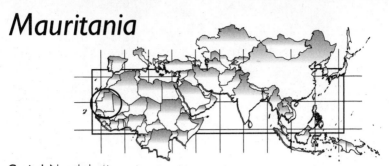

**Capital:** Nouakchott
**Population:** 2,700,000
**Language:** Arabic
**Major Religion:** Islam
**Major People Groups:** Bidan (White Moors), Maure (Black Moors),
   Arabized Berbers
**Strategic Town or City:** Atar

Mauritania is a large desert country located in northwest Africa, and is often covered in dust from frequent Saharan sandstorms. Mauritania is a multiracial nation and one of the most isolated countries in the world, dividing Arab North and Black West Africa. This area was once part of the powerful ancient African empires of Ghana and Mali. Arab invaders later overran these two empires, and still later the Portuguese set up trading posts along the coast, and the region gradually became a center for the slave trade. The territory came under French control in 1903, and Mauritania won its independence in November of 1960. The seventh holiest city of Islam, Chinguetti, is in the heart of Mauritania.

Despite the government's attempts to unify the nation, most Mauritanians remain fiercely loyal to family and ethnic ties rather than the nation. Up to 1970, about 70% of Mauritanians were nomadic. The Moors, descendants of the Arabs and Berbers, speak mainly Arabic. They take great pride in their Islamic heritage and are very hard to reach with the gospel. They view themselves as "keepers of the faith." Nevertheless, these people have tragically suffered through decades of drought, economic crisis, poverty, and hardship.

Marabouts (holy men) dominate and influence the Muslim population. They are the main source of magic charms, curses, and sorcery, giving them great power and prestige. The Hassanis are the warrior class, and at the bottom of the social structure are the Black Moors. Their forefathers were slaves who were adopted into Moor society. Although slavery became illegal at independence, it remains pervasive. Tens of thousands of people were still in positions of servitude in 1992.

Since independence, Mauritania has been an Islamic republic. At least two groups of the Islamic brotherhood are heavily into occult practices. One offshoot is the Hamallya, who emphasize equality (since most are the descendants of slaves), but they accentuate the most mystical Islamic beliefs. The other group is the Marabouts, who are often called upon to heal the sick.

No freedom of religion exists in Mauritania. All citizens by law are Sunni Muslims and are subject to shari'ah law. All evangelistic efforts are illegal, as is proselytization or conversion to another religion. Mauritanians wishing to accept Christ are subject to a death sentence according to law. There are very few known indigenous believers in Mauritania, but a few of the Christian fellowships are growing and showing signs of life.

According to several confidential sources, there are now two small house churches in the country. Yet, one missionary related that she feels she is not yet a harvester, or even breaking up the ground for sod, but a "stone-picker" to prepare the land. The major obstacles to ministry are laws with severe repercussions forbidding the renunciation of Islam, interracial tensions within the

stratified caste system, few Christian fellowships, and little or no
leadership for the believers.

## *Prayer Points*

⌣· Let us believe God that the Mauritanians will humble themselves and acknowledge their need for a Savior and forgiveness of sins. This may mean continued economic pressure on
   the Mauritanians. Whatever it takes, let us ask our loving
   Father to bring them to their knees so they will cry out to the
   one true God for salvation.

⌣· Ask the Lord to tear the blinders off the eyes of the Mauri-
   tanian peoples; maybe it will take visions of Jesus just like the
   one Saul of Tarsus had on the road to Damascus.

⌣· Many Mauritanians continue to live nomadic lifestyles; some
   are traders, spread out in Mali, Senegal, Gambia, Guinea,
   Guinea-Bissau, and Ivory Coast. Pray that these scattered,
   wandering people will be won to Christ and that they, in
   turn, will become itinerant evangelists, spreading the gospel
   wherever they go.

# Sudan

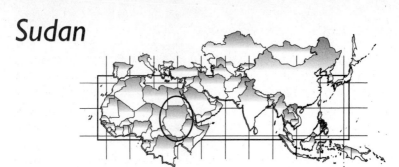

**Capital:** Khartoum
**Population:** 33,600,000
**Languages:** Arabic, Nubian, and many others
**Major Religions:** Islam, Animism, Roman Catholicism, Protestant
   Christianity
**Major People Groups:** Sudanese Arab, Dinka, Fur, Nuer
**Strategic Town or City:** Umm Durman

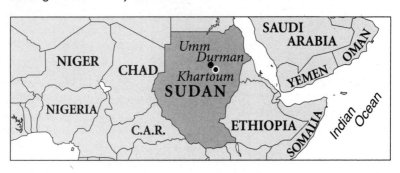

Since independence in 1956, Muslims in the north and Christians in the south have fought a long, bitter war for control of Sudan. The division has not been only along religious lines, but ethnic lines as well. A military coup in 1989 led to the establishment of a hard-line Islamic government. Since that time, shari'ah law has been imposed on the entire country and has led to an escalation of the fighting. Whole villages in the southern part of the country, under the control of the Christian minority, have been wiped out. In many instances, women and children have been taken captive and turned into slaves in the northern part of the country.

More than one million people have died due to starvation, martyrdom, and the fighting. Sudan is home to many thousands of dedicated Christians, but the war and the atrocities have made life unbelievably difficult for believers, especially those living in refugee camps. However, they are able to hold on in the midst of incredible difficulties because of their strong faith.

One missionary working beside the local believers in these difficult circumstances recently reported an incident that shows the faith of the Sudanese believers. They were in a refugee camp when planes from the north bombed their base of operations. The target of the bombs was an airstrip three miles away where approximately 100 children were working to improve the runway. The missionaries' first impulse was to rush to the site to see if anyone was hurt, but the national Christians immediately gathered to pray. While they were praying, word came that everyone was OK. The missionaries were humbled by the example of their Sudanese brothers and sisters who turned to God in a crisis rather than relying on human efforts.

Sudan is the largest nation in Africa, stretching more than 1,200 miles from north to south. It is home to over 140 ethnic groups, dominated by Muslim Arabs in the north and African Christians and animists in the south.

## Prayer Points

↳· Pray for the believers facing tremendous persecution and hardship. Ask the Holy Spirit to comfort and strengthen all those enduring the daily onslaught of war and torture. Ask God to break the hearts of believers all over the world to stand in prayer with those who are suffering terribly in refugee camps, both in Sudan and neighboring countries.

↳· Pray against the enemy and his evil plans to further war, persecution, and deception in Sudan. Pray for a righteous government to be installed.

↳· Ask our Father to use the horrible hardships in Sudan to reach many who would otherwise not hear the gospel.

↳· Pray for unity among the believers in the south, despite tribal and denominational differences.

⌣· Let us believe God for an end to the atrocities, the destruction of churches, massacres, murder of pastors and elders, and
   for a worldwide outcry to be raised up against what is happening in Sudan.
⌣· In the midst of the fighting, believe God for those who are
   unreached with the gospel to hear the good news and be
   saved, and for churches to be born out of the persecution that
   will stand firm in the midst of the fiery ordeal.

# Afghanistan

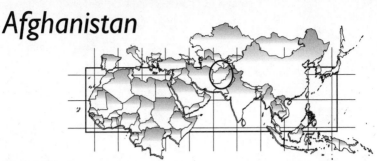

**Capital:** Kabul
**Population:** 25,400,000
**Languages:** Dari, Pushtu, and others
**Major Religion:** Islam
**Major People Groups:** Pushtun, Tajik, Hazara, Uzbek, Turkmen
**Strategic Town or City:** Qandahar

Afghanistan is a rugged, mountainous country that was once the fruit basket of Central Asia. A well-developed underground irrigation system supplied water from the Hindu Kush Mountains to the high desert plains, but that was all destroyed by Genghis Khan.

War has devastated Afghanistan. After a series of coups and countercoups, Soviet troops disguised as Afghan soldiers landed in Kabul (pronounced "cobble") in 1979. They were pushed out of the country in 1992 by a well-financed guerilla movement known as the mujahadin.

The withdrawal of the Soviet troops left a political vacuum that led to eight years of bloody civil war. The Iron Will of the Taliban, an Islamic fundamentalist movement begun amongst students and orphans, has been imposed on the people of Afghanistan with ferocious force and discipline.

Twenty-five nongovernment organizations (NGO) were forced out of the country in July 1998. For the first time since 1951 there were no Western believers serving in Afghanistan. Taliban threats to arrest Afghans associated with NGOs were carried out. Christian humanitarian organizations were unceremoniously forced out of the country after serving the Afghan people for 32 years.

Although the people of Afghanistan have been resistant to the gospel since their forced conversion to Islam in the seventh century A.D., many Afghans have questioned Islam because of the suffering they have experienced at the hands of fellow Muslims. This new openness has led to many Afghans coming to faith in Christ.

## *Prayer Points*

- Ask God for mercy for the Taliban leaders and for the veil of darkness over their eyes to be removed so they might see the truth of the gospel.
- Pray for Afghan believers to be strengthened and filled with courage as they face persecution and possible martyrdom.
- Pray that the hundreds of thousands of Afghan refugees living in camps along the Afghan-Pakistan border would hear the good news.
- Pray that Christian workers preparing to go would find a place of effective service.
- Pray for the Taliban movement to be exposed and to fall from power. Ask our Father in heaven to establish godly leaders over the nation.
- Intercede for the powers of fear and violence to be pulled down, and for dreams and visions of Jesus to be given to sincere seekers throughout the land.
- Pray against the government's ethnic cleansing against minority people groups.
- Pray for a Christian brother who has fled the country because of his faith; the government intends to take his life.

# Kuwait

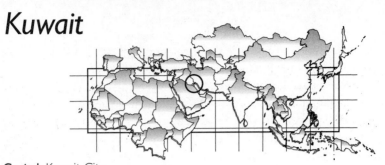

**Capital:** Kuwait City
**Population:** 2,900,000
**Languages:** Arabic, English
**Major Religions:** Islam, Hinduism
**Major People Groups:** Kuwaiti Arab, Arab
**Strategic Town or City:** Al-Ahmadi

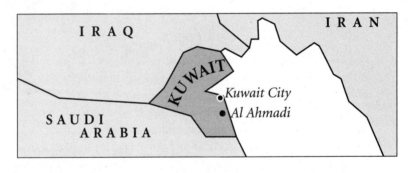

God is at work in Kuwait. Many Kuwaitis turned to God for help during the Gulf War, and still others became disillusioned with Islam because of the invasion by Iraq, their Muslim brothers. Some Kuwaiti believers dare to attend expatriate churches openly, but most are meeting in underground cell churches, studying the Bible and worshipping their newfound Lord.

Kuwait is governed by a sheik but is dominated by several small but very powerful families who control the economy of Kuwait. Since the war in 1991, the sheik and his family have responded to the demands for greater freedom. In the 1992 elections, the opposition gained a majority of seats in the newly re-established parliament. The cabinet is tightly controlled by the sheik.

In 1994 a report was received showing God's hand at work in the Kuwaiti parliament: "In a major and unexpected blow to Muslim fundamentalists, the Kuwaiti Parliament killed a bill to segregate male and female students in the classrooms, libraries, and restaurants in Kuwait University." The vote was indicative of the mood in Kuwait for change and gives insight into the struggle for control of Kuwait that is raging between Islamic fundamentalists and moderates.

After the war, thousands of Christian workers were able to enter and serve Kuwait in the rebuilding process. Kuwait had less than one million indigenous residents before the war, and many of those were killed, kidnapped, or wounded during the fighting. This has opened the door for people from all over the world to serve the people of Kuwait.

Westerners in general and Americans in particular have been hailed as heroes in Kuwait because they helped liberate the Kuwaiti people from Saddam Hussein.

## Prayer Points

- Pray for the prominent business families mentioned above, that they will be visited by the presence of God and many of them will see Jesus and accept Him as their Lord and Savior.
- Thank the Lord that in spite of the tremendous suffering that took place in the Gulf War, God has used it to bring many Kuwaitis to Himself. Pray that spiritual hunger will continue to grow in the hearts of the Kuwaiti people.
- Christian radio, video, and audio cassettes are important means of communicating the gospel within restrictive Kuwait. Pray that hearts will respond when they hear the gospel message.
- Pray that Kuwaiti businessmen will meet Christians as they travel to other countries. Pray for those Christians to speak boldly of their Savior.
- Ask God to strengthen the believers in Kuwait and that their faith will not fail.

# Bangladesh

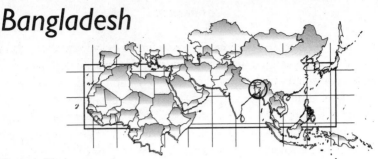

**Capital:** Dhaka
**Population** 146,600,000
**Languages:** Bengali, English, others
**Major Religions:** Islam, Hinduism, Buddhism
**Major People Groups:** Bengali, many tribal groups
**Strategic Town or City:** Satkhira

One of the greatest revivals ever to take place among Muslims coming to Christ has taken place in Bangladesh! Tens of thousands have received Christ, primarily among villagers and tribal groups. There continues to be great responsiveness to the gospel among the indigenous peoples of Bangladesh. One female medical worker has seen scores of Muslim women accept Christ through her clinic. Village workers have had open doors to preach the gospel, and whole villages have been swept into the kingdom.

This has not always been the case; Bangladesh has a long and bloody history. Along with the rest of the Indian subcontinent, the territory now comprising Bangladesh was part of British India until independence from India in 1947. Then Bangladesh was part of Pakistan, until it gained independence in 1971 following a bloody civil war. Bangladesh was primarily a Hindu country until mass conversion to Islam in the 13th century.

More than half the population of Bangladesh is under the age of 16, and though there is a great deal of unrest among the student population, there is also a tremendous openness to the gospel.

At the same time that Bangladesh has experienced spiritual blessings, there have also been upheavals in the nation—in both the political and natural realms. Typhoons have taken hundreds of thousands of lives. Coups, civil unrest, annual floods, overpopulation, and horrific poverty have plagued the people for many centuries. It is as if there is a curse over the land.

Let us join with millions of other praying Christians in one mighty voice for the peoples of Bangladesh, and for the bondage Satan holds over Bangladesh to be broken.

## Prayer Points

- Pray for indigenous Christian leaders to be strengthened, for wisdom, courage, and for the anointing of the Spirit to lead the church.
- Cry out to God for His Word to be disseminated, for the church to hunger for teaching in righteousness and truth, and for the Bible to be translated and spread in every language of the land.
- Intercede for the curse over Bangladesh to be broken through the prayers and repentance of God's people.
- Lift up the political leaders of Bangladesh to be moral, God-fearing, and free from corruption. Pray for humble leaders to bless the land by honest and righteous service to the people.
- Ask the Father for revival fires to spread through the nation; pray for missionaries to be united, for unnecessary disputes over doctrine to cease, and for the church to be one through the cross and repentance.
- Pray for church planters and pastors to be raised up for every people group, for every town and village, and for every urban neighborhood.

# Japan

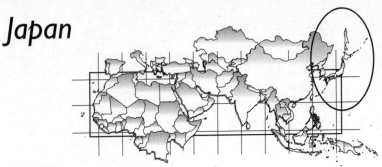

**Capital:** Tokyo
**Population:** 127,500,000
**Language:** Japanese
**Major Religions:** Shintoism, Buddhism
**Major People Group:** Japanese
**Strategic Town or City:** Osaka

One of the great myths of modern missions is the hardness of the Japanese people to the gospel. In reality, there is a curiosity and interest in Western things in the heart of the Japanese, which is a natural doorway to sharing the gospel of Christ.

Japanese youth are particularly open to change; one poll of university students showed that Christianity is admired and Jesus a respected figure. Typical of this openness is the testimony of a young man who accepted Christ while fishing after hearing the gospel from a missionary there with a short-term team. Today he is a "fisher of men" as a missionary to Central Asia, reaching Muslims for the Lord.

Japan is known as the the Land of the Rising Sun, because, as legend tells it, Japan was founded by Emperor Jimmu, a descendant of the sun goddess. Shintoism, an indigenous religious system, embraces the worship of emperors like Jimmu, ancestors, and nature. Japanese see their environment as a highly spiritual place animated by thousands of gods.

There are a little over one million believers in Japan, and the doors are wide open for English teachers and other missionaries who will serve Japanese people in practical ways.

There is a strong value on lordship in Japanese culture. The Samurai warriors would die for their lord; during WWII, Japanese soldiers died for their emperor; and now Japanese businessmen die for their companies. This is a cultural value that God could use to change the world if the Japanese were to turn their commitment to lordship to the King of Kings and Lord of Lords, Jesus Christ!

## *Prayer Points*

- Japan is in the midst of a major economic crisis, the outcome of which will affect millions of people. Pray for God to use this time of hardship to open the hearts of Japanese people to the gospel.
- Japan is deeply devoted to material prosperity and the development of business and technology. These are false gods who have betrayed the Japanese people. Pray for revelation to the hearts and minds of the leaders of the nation so that they will turn to the one true God.
- Intercede for the youth of Japan; they are the key to reaching the rest of the nation. Ask our Father to draw them to Himself as they turn from the values and ways of their parents' generation.
- The Japanese tend to see Christianity as a Western religion because many Japanese churches have adopted Western styles of worship and ministry. Pray for the Holy Spirit to inspire the hearts of Japanese Christians with indigenous forms of worship.
- Ask the Lord to open the eyes of Christian leaders in Japan to the blessing of servant leadership.
- Lift up this powerful nation; ask God to send revival to Japan. May His Spirit sweep the nation with a move of God that will impact the entire country and result in the conversion of millions of people.

# Guinea-Bissau

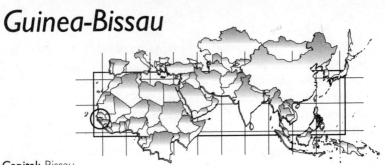

**Capital:** Bissau
**Population:** 1,200,000
**Language:** Portuguese
**Major Religions:** Animism, Islam
**Major People Groups:** Balanta, Fula, Mandingo
**Strategic Town or City:** Bissau

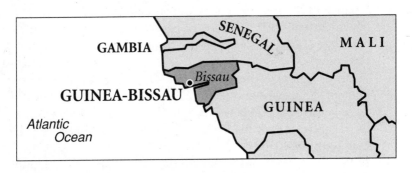

Located in West Africa, Guinea-Bissau is one of the world's poorest nations, with a debt/income ratio of almost three to one. The lack of substantial raw materials, devastation due to war, and socialistic policies have led to a lack of foreign investment in Guinea-Bissau, resulting in poor employment opportunities.

In 1879, the Portuguese took control of the region and profited from the wealth brought by trading gold, ivory, and slaves. This vile practice pitted tribe against tribe as Africans sold each other to slave traders. Guinea-Bissau was a Portuguese colony until 1974 when, after a devastating war, the nation gained its independence. One-party revolutionary regimes became the standard governing authorities until 1993.

On the spiritual front, Guinea-Bissau was influenced by the Catholic Church during Portuguese rule. Evangelicals were forbidden or discriminated against during that time period. Since independence, freedom for Christian activities has steadily increased, and visa restrictions for new Protestant agencies were relaxed in 1990. Even though Catholicism was the national religion for many years, animism and Islam are now the most widely practiced religions in Guinea-Bissau.

Currently there is openness to the gospel. The suffering experienced during the war for independence has drawn many to the freedom found only in Christ. The Catholic Church is still recovering from its association with the Portuguese colonial regime, while committed Christians have won a credibility that gives promise of an abundant harvest.

Worldwide Evangelization for Christ, International (WEC), was the only Protestant missionary organization allowed to work in the country from 1939–1990. Today, there are not many believers in Guinea-Bissau, but the leadership in the evangelical church is mature. Many believers have a great vision for evangelism and ministry outreach.

## Prayer Points

- Pray for a move of God's Spirit that results in tens of thousands of people coming to Christ.
- Guinea-Bissau is very poor, and the people suffer because of the poverty. Let us claim the promise of 2 Chronicles 7:14, asking God to move upon the people with a spirit of prayer and repentance that leads to healing for the land.
- Guinea-Bissau is on the brink of a move of God; let us press in through prayer, trusting God to send workers and break bondages so that His Son will be worshipped in every village and city in the nation. Let us believe God specifically for 100 new churches to be started in the next twelve months!
- Many of the 20 or so ethnic groups have no gospel witness. Pray that the gospel would be brought to them so that Jesus will receive the just reward of His suffering on their behalf: their obedience and worship.

# Bhutan

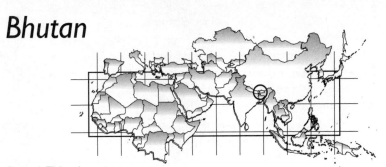

**Capital:** Thimphu
**Population:** 1,900,000
**Language:** Dzongka
**Major Religions:** Buddhism, Hinduism, Islam
**Major People Groups:** Drupka, Nepali
**Strategic Town or City:** Thimphu

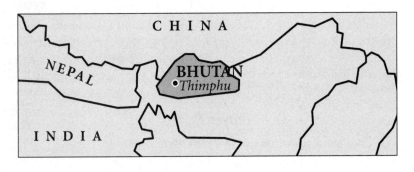

The tiny mountain kingdom of Bhutan is shrouded in secrecy and favors isolation from the rest of the world. Closed to all foreigners until 1974, Bhutan still prefers to keep visitors out. Frequent and very violent thunderstorms give this tiny nation its name, the Land of the Thunder Dragon.

The Drupka, or dragon people, are the majority people group of Bhutan. They dominate the government and are devout followers of Lamaistic Buddhism, the state religion. Evangelism or public expression of worship by any other faith is illegal. Though Bhutan is one of the most isolated countries in the world, much attention has been given to this tiny land, especially since the first Praying through the Window project in 1993.

There are no known Drupka believers. The majority of the population lives in valleys, each protected by its own guardian spirit.

Relentless prayer is needed for a breakthrough for Bhutan. God wants us to stand in united faith with all those praying through the window that Bhutan will experience a touch of the Spirit of the living God. Nothing is too hard for the Lord! No longer will Bhutan be without a church to worship the Lamb of God! It is God's promise. Scripture promises that every tribe and tongue will be around the throne of God (Rev. 5:9)!

## *Prayer Points*

- Let us turn the table in prayer on the government; it has persecuted Nepali believers in Bhutan and taken a strong stand against the gospel. Bless the government of Bhutan! Pray for the salvation of many in positions of authority.
- Ask God to give Buddhist spiritual leaders dreams and visions of the Lord Jesus and of the cross of Christ. The Holy Spirit does not need a passport, nor is He any man's debtor.
- Pray for Bhutanese students studying overseas, particularly in India, to hear the gospel and to receive it with open and glad hearts.
- Pray against satanic strongholds of fear, violence, and spiritual darkness and deception, that they will be broken!
- Believe God in prayer for an army of workers to be called to Bhutan and to respond in obedience to the prompting of the Holy Spirit.
- Ask the Lord to open doors for the *Jesus* film to be shown throughout Bhutan, particularly on television.

# Saudi Arabia

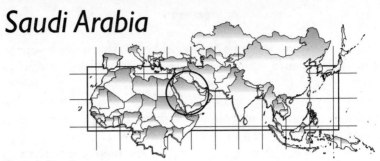

**Capital:** Riyadh
**Population:** 22,000,000
**Language:** Arabic
**Major Religion:** Islam
**Major People Groups:** Arab, Yemeni
**Strategic Town or City:** Jiddah

Saudi Arabia is the spiritual headquarters of Islam, the most influential religion in the world after Christianity. It was no accident that, during the Gulf War, God used Christians serving in the armed forces to spread the gospel in Saudi Arabia. As a result, there are hundreds of Saudi believers, including scores of underground churches.

The witness of the gospel has reached all the way to the royal family, including signs and wonders to confirm the preaching of God's Word. Some nomadic Saudi's have traveled many miles over desert expanses to hear the good news, while others have received it in written form. It is estimated that over 100,000 Bibles and New Testaments have been distributed in Saudi Arabia, and many more Christian books and tracts.

Saudi Arabia is one of the wealthiest countries in the world, containing about 25% of the world's oil reserves. This wealth has resulted in rapid economic and social development. The wealth of Saudi Arabia is used to spread the gospel of Islam. Muslim missionaries are sent all over the world, and Saudi oil money is used to build a mosque every five miles in East Africa.

Saudis are known for their self-confidence and generosity. Perhaps these qualities spring from their identity as "pure Arabs" and guardians of the holy cities of Islam, Medina, and Mecca. The entire Muslim world prays facing toward Mecca, the birthplace of the prophet Mohammed. Good Muslims are expected to make a *hajj* (pilgrimage) to Mecca at least once in their lifetime.

The Bible promises that God's Word will not return void; let us pray fervent, desperate prayers today for His Word to penetrate the heart and mind of every man and woman living in the Saudi kingdom. When we look at the rise of Islamic fundamentalism, or focus our attention on Muslim extremists, we allow our faith to diminish and we begin to see Muslim "terrorists" as our enemies. Indeed they may act as enemies of the gospel, but God is in the business of redeeming the enemies of the cross and turning them into ministers of reconciliation. With this in mind, let us enter into prayer for Saudi Arabia with an attitude of humility and openness to God concerning any attitudes we may need to change.

## Prayer Points

- Let us begin by repenting of any fear, hatred, or bitterness toward Muslims in general, or Saudi Arabians in particular: "Create in me a clean heart, O Lord."
- Ask God to break your heart over the lostness of Saudi Arabians who will spend eternity in hell if they do not hear the good news of the gospel.
- Lift up the royal family of Saudi Arabia; there are more than 5,000 princes in the royal family. May the gospel reach each one of them and their families, and may the Spirit of the living God penetrate each heart with conviction of sin, awareness of the need for forgiveness, and a revelation of

God's gracious offer of mercy through our Lord Jesus Christ. Pray for dreams and visions of Jesus in all His radiance and glory!

⌣· Pray for divine protection for the believers, and that the eyes of their family members and the secret police will be blinded (when necessary) to Bibles, prayer meetings, and the discipling of new believers.

⌣· Ask the Father to create more opportunities for church planting in Saudi Arabia so that His Son will be worshipped by small but faithful bands of disciples in every village, clan, and family in the land!

# Guinea

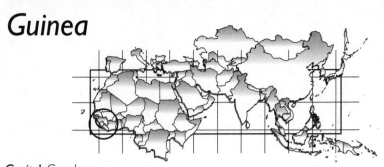

**Capital:** Conakry
**Population:** 9,200,000
**Language:** French
**Major Religion:** Islam
**Major People Groups:** Fula, Maninka, Susu
**Strategic Town or City:** Labe

Guinea is a small country located in West Africa and remains one of Africa's least evangelized nations. However, since 1991 there has been a growing freedom to worship and evangelize. Guinea's only real financial support comes from the Muslim nation of Saudi Arabia. Civil unrest between tribes is potentially explosive. Also, government red tape has been making land ownership very difficult for the people. Travel in Guinea is very primitive and difficult.

The great medieval empires of Ghana, Mali, and Songhai ruled what is now Guinea and brought prosperity to West Africa. When Portuguese explorers came to the region in the 15th century, they found Guinea to be rich in a great variety of natural resources. In 1895, as French Guinea, the country became part of French West Africa. Slave trade prospered during the years of French domination. The first president after independence in 1958, Ahmed Sekou Toure, formed a single-party socialist state, which led to increasingly repressive laws and economic collapse.

When Toure died in 1984, a military group seized power and basic freedoms were restored. The government has struggled to bring economic recovery. However, with fertile land and abundant mineral resources, Guinea is potentially one of the richest countries in West Africa. A revival of interest in the occult, animism, and Islam hinders the spread of the gospel.

## *Prayer Points*

⌣· Pray that demonic strongholds over Guinea will be pulled down and that righteousness will rule the nation.

⌣· The Christian minority lacks zeal for the lost and compassion for their Muslim neighbors; pray for a revival in the church.

⌣· Ask the Lord to send missionaries and Christian workers from Nigeria and other African nations with the gospel.

⌣· Ask the Lord to bring reconciliation and stability to the 40 ethnic groups, and wisdom and righteousness to their leaders.

⌣· Lift up the believers; many are struggling with poverty and disease. May God comfort and heal His people in Guinea, even as we pray!

⌣· Ask the Lord to impart a vision for the nations to the people of Guinea and to give them faith to have an impact on the whole earth!

# Thailand

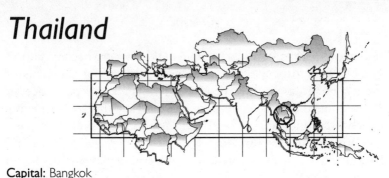

**Capital:** Bangkok
**Population:** 63,700,000
**Language:** Thai
**Major Religions:** Buddhism, Islam
**Major People Groups:** Thai, Chinese, Malay, Khmer
**Strategic Town or City:** Sonkhla

Thailand is known for its military coups, prostitution, and Buddhist temples. Thailand's capital, Bangkok, is famous for its immoral nightlife and rampant prostitution that attracts tourists from all over the world. Prostitution rings buy village boys and girls from poor parents lured by false promises and easy money. These children are used until they are too old or contract AIDS. One Christian ministry actually buys back the children sold into prostitution, then cares for them through a long period of restoration.

Tens of thousands of Thai have come to Christ through the sacrificial efforts of missionaries over many years. There is tremendous interest in spiritual things among university students.

One church planting team has won over 100 students to Christ in the last three years through short-term outreaches!

However, the majority of the Thai people have never heard the gospel even once. Compared to the huge population, the number of Christians is tiny. By nature, the Thai people are gentle, but can store hurts and offenses in their hearts for years, then suddenly explode in outbursts of anger and violence. It is important for us to stand with our Thai brothers and sisters as we join hearts in prayer, especially for unity in the church and for reconciliation where there are broken relationships.

## Prayer Points

- Ask God for millions of Thai to hear the gospel and to respond positively. Ask God to show you ways He wants to touch the hearts of the Thai people, then pray accordingly.
- Lift up the hundreds of thousands of village young people sold into prostitution each year. Believe God in prayer that He will heal their wounded hearts, renew their minds, and wash them by His blood. Storm heaven for divine intervention to bring prostitution to an end in Thailand!
- Pray for every Buddhist temple in Thailand to be filled with the presence of the living God; ask God to reveal Himself in dreams and visions to sincere seekers. Lift up the church in Thailand, especially that more Thai pastors and evangelists will be raised up.
- Thank God for the years of selfless service of missionaries who have labored in Thailand over the past 150 years. Give thanks that so many Thai have found Christ and that many more will still come to Christ.
- Praise God for over 30 churches started by short-term teams working in the northern part of the country with a career missionary.

# Niger

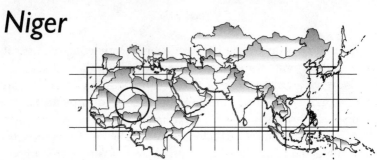

**Capital:** Niamey
**Population:** 11,100,000
**Languages:** French, Hausa
**Major Religions:** Islam, animism
**Major People Groups:** Hausa, Djerma, Sokoto Fulani, Tuareg
**Strategic Town or City:** Zinder

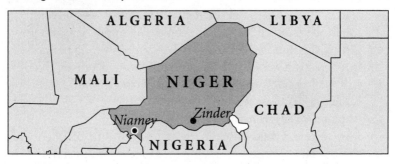

Plagued by poverty and hopelessness, Niger is said to be the poorest country in West Africa. Niger gained independence from France in 1960. A military regime ruled between 1974 and 1991. In 1992, Niger adopted a multiparty constitution.

Many residents live in remote areas. The desert conditions and poor roads make travel difficult. Some regions of Niger still remain virtually untouched by the gospel, even though low-key evangelism faces few restrictions. The people of Niger are ashamed of the malnutrition, disease, and poverty that have devastated their nation. They are in desperate need of the hope and joy that comes only from knowing Jesus Christ.

Over 80% of Niger's population is Muslim, although many are only nominal in their faith. Animism is also widely practiced, especially at the nation's centers for Islamic learning: the city of Say and the Village of Lugn.

Cultural barriers create strife and prejudice between many tribal groups, and the relationships between missionaries and nationals are strained as well. Traditional forms of evangelism are very difficult because only 10% of Niger's residents can read.

Poverty and famine have taken a terrible toll on Niger. In some areas, the majority of the population has no food and each morning families must travel several miles looking for a precious, nourishing shrub called *anza*.

Food distribution is insufficient, and many old people and children die of malnutrition and infectious diseases. Mothers look on helplessly as their babies grow weaker.

While Niger's people are free to change religions, few have responded to the gospel. The Tuareg people, a nomadic Muslim group in North Niger, and the Wodaabe people, an animistic group, have some Christians among them, but they will not respond in significant numbers to Christ unless there is a major breakthrough.

A group of elders in one village has asked for a missionary to come and live among them so they can learn about Jesus. So far, after asking almost three years ago, there is no one who will accept the invitation.

## Prayer Points

⌣· Ask the Lord of the Harvest to raise up workers to go to Niger, especially to the village that has asked for a missionary to tell them about Jesus.

⌣· There is freedom to evangelize in Niger, but there is also persecution against those who do so. Pray for the believers to be strengthened in their faith and bold to tell others about Jesus.

⌣· The Tuareg, Fulani, and Hausa are all unreached tribal peoples in Niger. They live in very remote locations and there is no church among them. Pray for a hunger for the gospel and for laborers to go to them.

⌣· The religious freedom given by the government means that missionaries can enter the land and help the people through social welfare programs. Ask Jesus to call people to go to serve the poor and preach the good news. The Lamb of God is worthy of the worship of all the peoples of Niger!

# Kyrgyzstan

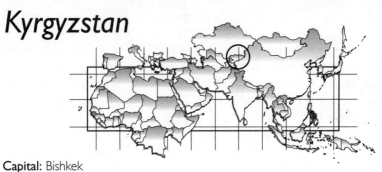

**Capital:** Bishkek
**Population:** 4,600,000
**Languages:** Kyrgyz, Russian
**Major Religions:** Islam, Russian Orthodoxy
**Major People Groups:** Kyrgyz, Russian, Uzbek, Dugan
**Strategic Town or City:** Osh

Kyrgyzstan is the most democratic of the former Soviet republics. Russia ruled Central Asia for 70 years, during which time they divided the land and peoples into six different republics. Since their independence in 1991, Kyrgyzstan has welcomed Western influence and economic investment with open arms.

The Kyrgyz people make up about 60% of the total population of Kyrgyzstan, with ethnic Russians making up another 21%. Although the capital, Bishkek, has been Russified, village life is still very conservative and experiencing a resurgence of Islam.

Kyrgyzstan is a springboard for reaching the other Central Asian republics because of its central location and freedom of religion. There were only 9 known believers in 1991, but today there are between 1,500 and 2,000 Kyrgyz who are following Christ, while many more made professions of faith in mass crusades held soon after Kyrgyzstan gained independence.

The Kyrgyz people are gentle, hospitable, and peace loving. Their mythical hero, Minaas, is celebrated in an epic poem that alludes back to a period when the Kyrgyz were nomads and warriors. The ancestors of the Kyrgyz and other Turkic peoples of Central Asia are the Mongols.

Kyrgyzstan is called the Switzerland of Central Asia because of the beautiful Tian Shan Mountains, "the Celestial Peaks." This is a strategic time in the history of Kyrgyzstan. Various political and religious forces are vying for influence, and the church is desperate for help. Church leaders want outside input but are leery of those with their own agendas. One Kyrgyz pastor has appealed for businessmen to help train church members in small business skills. Others have appealed for teachers of English to go to all 49 of the administrative districts of Kyrgyzstan; the doors are wide open.

## Prayer Points

⌣· Pray for Kyrgyz church leaders to be strengthened and to be discerning as outside influences pour into the land.

⌣· Ask the Holy Spirit to raise up church planters to pioneer self-multiplying church planting movements.

⌣· Cry out to God for teachers of English to go to all of the 49 administrative districts in Kyrgyzstan.

⌣· Intercede for the government to resist efforts on the part of the Turkish, Uzbek, and Saudi Arabian governments to turn Kyrgyzstan into an Islamic state.

⌣· Believe God for revival to sweep over the Kyrgyz church with holiness, purity, and boldness. Pray for the church leaders to be filled with the Holy Spirit.

⌣· Pray for unity among the Christians from other lands that are serving in Kyrgyzstan; ask the Father to daily renew their love for the Kyrgyz people and for a spirit of humility and brokenness among them.

# Iran

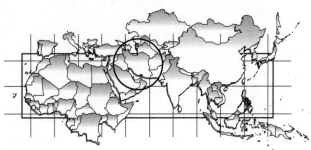

**Capital:** Tehran
**Population:** 75,700,000
**Languages:** Farsi, Turkish, Turkmen, Kurdish
**Major Religion:** Islam
**Major People Groups:** Persian, Azerbaijani, Kurd, Luri, Gilaki, Mazanderani, Turkmen
**Strategic Town or City:** Mashhad

The former president of Algeria, Ahmed Ben Bella, once said about the Ayatollah Khomeini of Iran, "A bright light appeared in Iran which illuminated the whole Muslim world." Soon after the return of Khomeini to Iran, a spirit of violence erupted in the Muslim world. A Muslim saying states, "One must wash blood with blood."

The Islamic revolution of 1979 in Iran revived radical Islam on a worldwide scale. This revival of fundamentalist Islam was aided by other factors but was led by Khomeini in Iran. Sadly, the new tyranny in Iran has turned out to be as cruel and corrupt as the dictatorship it replaced.

The followers of Khomeini are Shiite Muslims, those devotees of Muhammad who also owe allegiance to Hussein, the grandson of Muhammad. In A.D. 680, Hussein was assassinated along with 72 of his followers. Shiite Islam looks to Hussein as an example of justice and the uncompromising battle against wicked rulers. Shiites want justice, and they are willing to shed their own blood to have it.

The church in Iran has suffered greatly under the murderous hands of Khomeini and his fanatical followers. Many have been martyred for their faith in Christ. In spite of this persecution, the church has grown by 800% since the Iranian revolution began in 1979! Of the estimated 40,000 believers in Iran, over one-third are converted Muslims.

Iran is the spiritual descendent of the ancient kingdom of Persia, which ruled a vast empire stretching from India to Egypt. In the seventh century, Arab armies overran Iran and Islam became the state religion.

The discovery of oil in Iran in the early 1900s made it possible for the Shiite revolution to be financed and exported, mainly in the form of political terrorism.

The battle for Iran is by no means over. The enemy wants us to think he owns Iran and that radical Islam is an unconquerable foe, but that is a lie.

Iran is not our enemy, Satan is. During this time of prayer for the 10/40 Window, let us heap blessings on Iran through spiritual warfare and prayer. Let us bless the people of Iran and pray that many of its leaders will find Christ. As we respond in the opposite spirit to violence and intimidation, we pave the way for the Holy Spirit to touch the hearts of millions of Iranians and prepare their hearts to hear the gospel of the Lord Jesus Christ! Jesus is Lord!

## Prayer Points

- The church in Iran is under attack. Pray for comfort, strength, and grace to endure persecution, threats, and lies.
- Lift up the 60,000 villages of Iran, that Jesus will be made known to every villager in their own language.

⌣· Pray that God will continue to speak to Iranians through dreams and visions. Ask God to pour out His Spirit so that hundreds of thousands of Iranians will come to Christ.

⌣· Pray for the Holy Spirit to infiltrate the upper ranks of the religious clergy so that many Muslim clerics will come to Christ.

⌣· Ask God to bring an end to the influence of Shiite Islam and to stop the spread of hate and violence through its adherents. Just as God brought down Communist governments two decades ago, ask Him to do it again in the Muslim world!

⌣· Pray that the hundreds of thousands of Muslim young people who are disillusioned with Islam and looking for a new way would find the Way, the Truth, and the Life in Jesus Christ.

# Burkina Faso

**Capital:** Ouagadougou
**Population:** 12,500,000
**Language:** French
**Major Religions:** Islam, traditional religions
**Major People Groups:** Mossi, Gurma, Dagaari
**Strategic Town or City:** Bobo-Dioulasso

Without the intervention of God, there is little hope for the nation of Burkina Faso. Located in West Africa, Burkina Faso is void of any seaports and prone to drought and famine. The Burkinabé people have a literacy rate of only 13%, and many must grow their own food just to survive. The spiritual and economic outlook is bleak, but there are some spiritual stirrings.

Christianity is beginning to grow. Since the latest coup in 1987, some policies restricting religion have been relaxed. The latest regime is more welcoming of the gospel, missionaries, and Christian aid programs. An exciting example of this freedom was demonstrated in October 1993. About 5,000 believers in Burkina Faso from various denominations came together to fast and pray for their country and other 10/40 Window countries. Also, on the country's National Day, 10,000 Bible portions were distributed at a parade. Response was so great that those wanting more followed the people who were distributing the material!

While God's Spirit is moving in Burkina Faso, there are major spiritual strongholds in the hearts and minds of the people. The Burkinabé people are influenced by a spirit of confusion in the political arena, the prevalence of occult practices in many of the 72 people groups, and violence in festivals and worship of crocodile and fish gods.

Like its neighbor, Benin, Burkina Faso gained independence from France in 1960. However, Burkina Faso has not experienced a transfer of power to a multiparty system of government. The military regimes that have governed Burkina Faso have brought much economic hardship, and the Burkinabé have endured extreme governmental policies, especially in the area of religion. The current regime characterizes itself as "revolutionary, democratic, anti-imperialist, and secular."

Similar to many other African nations, Burkina Faso is heavily influenced by the traditional religions of its people. Animism is still practiced among some tribes. Islam, which claimed only 10% of the population in 1900, now accounts for approximately 48% of the people who claim religious affiliation. Today, Islam continues to grow rapidly in many areas of Burkina Faso. But Burkina Faso holds much hope for seeing many more respond to the truth of Jesus Christ.

## Prayer Points

- ⌣· The doors are open to this struggling but responsive 10/40 Window country; pray for more laborers to respond to the Lord of the Harvest!
- ⌣· Intercede for literacy workers so the percentage of people able to read God's Word in their own language will increase.
- ⌣· Pray for the believers to mature and for Bible teachers and mentors who will invest in the lives of the church leaders and Christian workers.

- Stand against the demonic strongholds of witchcraft and animism that grip the hearts of the people. Ask God to deliver people from secret societies, idolatry, and fetishism.
- Ask God to bless and heal the land and to send revival to Burkina Faso. Lift up the political leaders and ask God to bless and keep them and put the fear of the Lord in their hearts and minds as they lead the nation.

# Mali

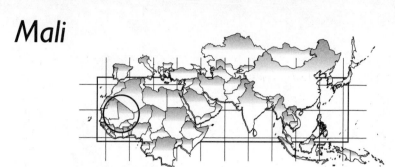

**Capital:** Bamako
**Population:** 10,700,000
**Language:** French
**Major Religion:** Islam
**Major People Groups:** Bambara, Fula Macina, Senufo
**Strategic Town or City:** Segou

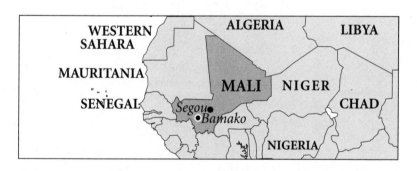

Have you ever heard of Timbuktu, or wondered where it is? This ancient city is located in north central Mali, on the Niger River, bordering the Sahara Desert. Timbuktu is an important trade city, a crossroads for Arabia and Black Africa.

At the zenith of Mali's power as a nation, it was one of the world's leading suppliers of gold. This attracted the attention of European colonizers, including the French, who built waterways and railroads to export goods more easily.

Mali gained independence from France in 1960. In 1991, a popular uprising overthrew the military dictatorship and replaced it with a multiparty democracy. Since the 1970s, drought has dev-astated Mali's largely agricultural economy and the nation has been plagued by famine. Corruption and mismanagement by dictatorships have worsened the economic hardship. Mali's infant mortality rate—173 deaths per 1,000 births—is among the highest in the world, and its gross national product—$300 per capita—places it among the world's 10 poorest nations.

Eight out of ten Malians are Muslim. Like other Islamic nations, Mali is dominated by radical Muslims who despise Christianity and are willing to die trying to obliterate it.

Muslim radicals sometimes come into Mali from Northern Africa to stir up intolerance of Christians and call for people to pledge their lives to see prominent Christians killed. Freedom of religion is staunchly maintained by the government, despite Muslim pressures to stop Christian missionary work.

Most Malians are moderate in their religious beliefs and tolerant of the Christian message. However, in some quarters there is suspicion of Christianity, a feeling that has been intensified by insensitive actions of some believers in the past. More recently, Christian workers have been restricted from working in certain areas, and in one instance, the home of a national pastor came under gunfire. However, the government of Mali welcomes Christian workers and is seeking to contain those who are opposing Christianity.

A literacy rate of only 10% makes evangelism through traditional means difficult, but missionaries using the *Jesus* film have had success in some parts of Mali. Bible translation work is in progress in at least ten languages. One mission has announced that in the 18 churches they planted in one year with over 1,000 converts, there are only 20 literate people. Doors in Mali appear to be open but could slam shut if fundamentalist Muslims continue to draw people to Islam. The Body of Christ in Mali must become unified and be covered with intercessory prayer so they can stand against great adversity.

Christian programs on Radio Bamako and ELWA have a wide audience and have opened many unreached villages to the gospel. In the past, national television has regularly offered Christians free television time.

## *Prayer Points*

⌣· Ask God to raise up church planters who are trained to serve as community development workers. There is a tremendous need to integrate evangelism and practical service for the poor.

⌣· Although Mali has no official restriction on evangelism, few missionaries are working in Mali. The conditions are hard, and the country is poor. Pray for those willing to lay down their lives for the sake of the glory of God in Mali!

⌣· Pray for the Spirit of God to move over the nation of Mali! Through prayer we can invade every level of Malian society and every part of the country. Most of the people in Mali have never heard the name of Jesus.

⌣· At the same time that we ask God to move in Mali, let us also trust Him to plant in the hearts of Malian believers the dream that is in His heart: that Jesus will be worshipped by every tribe and tongue and people and nation. The Lamb is worthy!

# Azerbaijan

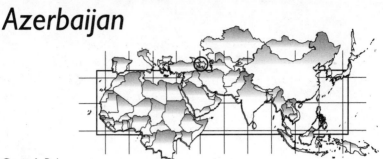

**Capital:** Baku
**Population:** 7,600,000
**Languages:** Azerbaijani, Russian, Armenian
**Major Religion:** Islam
**Major People Groups:** Azeri, Russian, Armenian
**Strategic Town or City:** Gjandza

The dominant political and economic factor in Azerbaijan today is the war with Armenia that has been fought off and on since 1988. Each nation claims a mountainous region called the Nagorno-Karabakh. Over a million Azeri have been displaced because of the war that has filled the capital, Baku, with refugees and displaced persons.

The Azerbaijani people evolved as migrating Turks intermarried with native Persians. Azerbaijan was assimilated into the Soviet Union and then received its freedom from Russia in 1991, after the breakup of the former Soviet Union.

The Communist regime tried to stamp out all vestiges of Islam, and almost succeeded. Since independence, however, Islam has experienced a resurgence.

There is very little freedom of religion, so what few Christians there are may not worship openly. However, the church is growing and there are opportunities for people from other lands to serve in this remote land. May God use our prayers for the Azerbaijani church and people to make a difference! Ask big things of God—nothing is too hard for Him!

## Prayer Points

⌣· Pray for the church to be strengthened and purified. Stand with the church that the Holy Spirit will anoint them for a powerful witness and that a mission movement will begin in Azerbaijani believers and spread to other nations!

⌣· Pray for the *Jesus* film to have a mighty effect on nonbelievers.

⌣· Lift up government leaders before God. Pray that they will be blessed, that they will be protected from dishonest people, and that they will be given wisdom by God to serve their people.

⌣· Pray for peace between Azerbaijan and Armenia. Ask the Lord for a just and final peace between these two nations, and ask Him to comfort those who have lost loved ones.

⌣· Intercede for a revival in Azerbaijan, for many thousands of souls to be saved, and for the spontaneous multiplication of churches to spread through the land.

# Benin

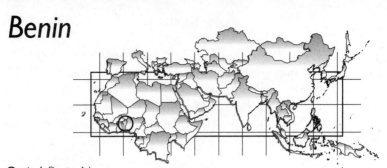

**Capital:** Porto-Novo
**Population:** 6,600,000
**Languages:** French, Fon, Yoruba, Dendi, and 49 others
**Major Religions:** Animism, Islam, Roman Catholicism
**Major People Groups:** Fon, Adja, Bariba, Yoruba, and 50 other African tribes
**Strategic Town or City:** Cotonou

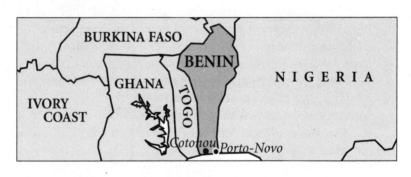

Small, obscure Benin was once home to one of the largest slave trade operations in West Africa and was known as "The Slave Coast." By the late 17th century, the Dahomey people were raiding their neighbors for slaves to sell to European traders. Benin, occupied by France until 1960, has been plagued by instability caused by economic problems, ethnic rivalries, and social unrest. A coup in 1972 brought in a Marxist-Leninist military government led by Lt. Col. Kerekou, who ruled as a virtual dictator until 1991. In recent years, a pluralistic constitution was adopted and legislative and presidential elections were held, but the elected government rests on uneasy alliances.

There is complete religious freedom in Benin, which is sub–Saharan Africa's least-evangelized non-Muslim country.

Benin has Africa's highest percentage of followers of traditional religions similar to voodoo. The well-educated and influential Fon people have led the country in ancestor worship and devotion to fetishes. They believe that God created hundreds of supernatural powers that affect human life and must be appeased and guarded against through their practices.

## Prayer Points

- Ask God to reveal Jesus to the leaders of the government in Benin. God can speak through dreams and visions; may He use these and other signs and wonders to turn the government leaders to Himself.
- Since 1987, both evangelicals and Catholics have experienced rapid church growth. Ask the Lord to raise up thousands more leaders with maturity and vision, equipped by God to minister to believers and nonbelievers alike in Benin.
- Ask the Lord of the Harvest to raise up laborers to take advantage of the freedom in Benin to preach the gospel and serve the poor.
- Join your prayers that God will bring about a just, democratic government for the people of Benin.
- Beseech God that the power of voodoo and occult practices will be exposed for what they are, and that the people of Benin will be free from demonic bondage. Jesus Christ is Lord!

# Indonesia

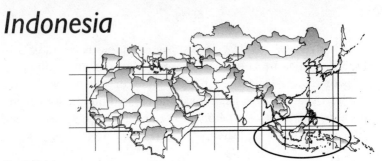

**Capital:** Jakarta
**Population:** 223,800,000
**Languages:** Indonesian, Malay, Chinese, English, and almost 700 tribal languages
**Major Religions:** Islam, Christianity, Hinduism, some Chinese religions
**Major People Groups:** Javanese, Sudanese, Madurese, Minang Kabau, Aceh, and many others
**Strategic Town or City:** Surabaya

More than ten million Muslims have come to Christ in Indonesia in the last 25 years! One missionary planted 49 churches in just eleven years through training Bible school students to plant churches on their weekends. Another Bible school requires each student to plant a church as a requirement for graduation!

There are over 13,000 islands in the Indonesian archipelago, stretching through Southeast Asia like a crescent moon. The Spice Islands, as they are called, have attracted adventurers and explorers for many centuries, from Marco Polo and Ferdinand Magellan, to Portuguese and Dutch colonialists.

Muslim mystics brought Islam to the Indonesian islands in the 13th century. Today, Indonesia is home to more Muslims than the entire Middle East.

In order to try and manage the diversity of peoples, languages, islands, and religious convictions, the government has put religious restrictions in place. Every citizen must profess one of five religions; tribal religions and animism are not allowed. Christianity is one of those religions and has grown the fastest. Amazing movements to Christ have taken place in Sumatra, Java, and Kalimantan. There has been a backlash from the Muslims, including riots, persecution, and destruction of some churches.

What God has done in Indonesia builds faith in our hearts for the rest of the Muslim world. Nothing is too difficult for God!

## Prayer Points

- Seven centuries ago the Acehnese people influenced many Indonesians to follow Islam. Pray that today they would come to Christ in great numbers and bring the gospel to many other peoples.
- Lift up the Minang Kabau, one of the more resistant people groups in the Indonesian islands.
- The government continues to hinder Christians and the spread of the gospel. Missionary visas are severely restricted, and a blind eye is turned to religious discrimination and persecution. Ask God to rule and overrule in the affairs of government in Indonesia. Pray that this trend would be reversed, that the gospel might be freely proclaimed in Indonesia.
- Lift up the Indonesian church, especially that it would see its responsibilities to reach other nations and peoples with the gospel.
- Pray for revival in nominal churches: for separation from animism and repentance for godless forms of religion. Many churches in Indonesia stretch back over a hundred years and desperately need revival.

# Laos

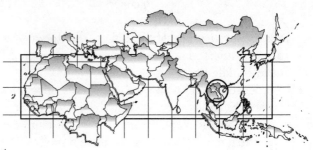

**Capital:** Vientiane
**Population:** 5,000,000
**Languages:** Lao, French, English
**Major Religions:** Buddhism, animism
**Major People Groups:** Lao, Hmong, Khmu, Tai, So
**Strategic Town or City:** Savannakhet

The Hmong people of Laos have been the target of political manipulation and abuse for many years. During the Vietnam War, the CIA used the Hmong as their ground troops to fight the Vietnamese, but then abandoned them when the war was over.

The Communist Lao People's Democratic Republic came into power in 1975, forcing many Laotians to flee to Thailand. The new government launched a program to convert Laos into a socialist country, starting with regulating all mass media, arresting those in opposition, and using military force to control and forcibly relocate dissidents, notably the Hmong people. These efforts failed, and the government was forced to decentralize control and encourage free enterprise.

Formerly part of French Indochina, Laos did not exist as a distinct territory until 1907. Ethnic Lao, related to the Thai people, make up about half the population. Minorities include ethnic Thai and Chinese, as well as a number of tribal mountain groups.

The gospel has not made a significant breakthrough in Laos, though efforts are still underway to translate, print, and distribute scripture portions in the various languages of Laos. Christianity is seen as a foreign religion and a threat to national security.

Buddhism is the greatest spiritual and ideological force in Laos. It is the driving force in Lao culture and remains a major influence in everyday life and a symbol of national identity. Offerings made at village altars and homes throughout the country owe their origin to an older animistic cult called Phi.

It is time to stir up our faith for Laos! This beautiful mountain country is long overdue for a visitation from heaven. As you pray for Laos, remember, millions of other Christians are also praying. Let us join our hearts in united, fervent prayers that the God of heaven will break through in Laos! He is able!

## Prayer Points

- Pray for the Hmong and other tribal groups that have been used by political forces from the West and the East. Many are scattered as refugees. May God reveal Himself to them as their comfort and refuge; they are far from their physical home in the mountains of Laos.
- Ask God to shake the tiny nation so that everyone knows that their true enemy is Satan and his demonic forces. May God open the eyes of the government leaders to see!
- Pray for those who are called and committed to Laos. Ask God to add many more laborers to their numbers, even right now as we intercede.
- Lift up the Bible translators and their efforts to translate, print, and distribute God's Word.
- The church is small, but it has been faithful in spite of persecution and isolation. Lift up the weak knees and drooping arms of our Christian brothers and sisters in Laos. May the God of all comfort reveal Himself to them today. They are not alone!

# Western Sahara

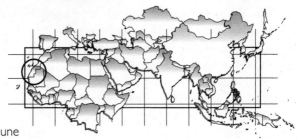

**Capital:** Laayoune
**Population:** 223,000
**Languages:** Arabic, Spanish, French
**Major Religion:** Islam
**Major People Groups:** Saharawi, Berber, Arab
**Strategic Town or City:** Laayoune

Months of planning and a year of secretive travel were required to deliver a single Bible to a new believer in Western Sahara. This precious copy of God's Word passed through four countries on its clandestine journey in the hands of two couriers. These courageous believers risked detection at many police checkpoints in their commitment to see their sister in Christ spiritually nourished by her own copy of the Word of God.

Formerly known as Spanish Sahara, Western Sahara is a vast desert land. Blazing hot summers, cold nights, desert sandstorms, and arid conditions make life in the unending desert expanses difficult.

War has raged in the Western Sahara since 1975, when Spain relinquished colonial control. Western Sahara is now claimed by

Morocco, and as of the publication of this prayer guide, the country is not recognized as an independent nation.

Saharawi freedom fighters, financed by Algeria and influenced by Communist ideology, have fought a long, bitter struggle for independence. Known as the Polisario Front, the freedom fighters have fought Spain, Morocco, and Mauritania, all having claimed the Western Sahara. A referendum negotiated by former US Secretary of State James Baker under the auspices of the United Nations was scheduled for late 1998.

Morocco has invested heavily in Western Sahara, building roads, hospitals, schools, and housing. Morocco has also flooded Western Sahara with its own people, hoping to influence the outcome of the referendum.

Tens of thousands of Saharawi have fled to refugee camps in Algeria. A few thousand more are scattered throughout Spain and the Canary Islands.

Visitors to Western Sahara are followed, and contacts with the local people are closely monitored. Conditions are oppressive for this relatively unknown people.

Until the early 1990s there were no known Saharawi believers. And though there are now several Saharawi who have professed Christ, they are unable to meet together, and most do not know about each other.

There is a handful of Christian workers committed to reaching the Saharawi—praise God they have responded to God's call. But they are few in number, poorly financed, and needing encouragement. Let us remember these Saharawi believers in prayer. The Lord loves the Saharawi, and through our prayers we can change the spiritual climate over this beautiful desert land!

## Prayer Points

- Pray with compassion and urgency for the Father's love to be revealed to this little known but not forgotten people.
- Lift up the tiny group of believers to be strengthened and filled with faith.

- ⌣· Cry out to the Lord of the Harvest for more workers to join the small team of Christians from different lands already committed to reaching the Saharawi.
- ⌣· Believe God for political and spiritual freedom from oppression and for God-fearing leaders to be raised up to lead the Saharawi.
- ⌣· Pray for churches to be established among the Saharawi in Spain and the Canary Islands, and for the new believers to boldly take the gospel to their native land.
- ⌣· Pray for the spirit of suspicion and oppression to be broken over the land. Also pray that those who are called would not give up in the face of fear and very difficult circumstances. There is nothing too hard for God!

# Egypt

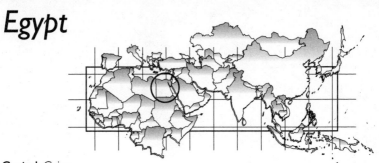

**Capital:** Cairo
**Population:** 69, 000,000
**Language:** Arabic
**Major Religions:** Islam, Coptic Christianity, and a small but growing number of evangelical believers
**Major People Groups:** Egyptian, Arabic, Nubian, Berber, and Bedouin
**Strategic Town or City:** Alexandria

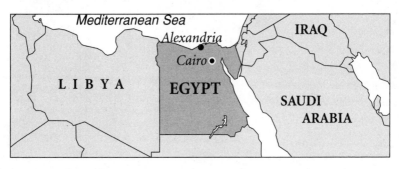

Egypt is a land of contrasts: wealth and poverty, openness to the gospel and Islamic fundamentalism, and urban cosmopolitan culture and village conservatism. The Land of the Pharaohs attracts archaeologists and tourists from all over the world. The wonder of the pyramids and sphinxes demonstrate the power of past Egyptian civilizations that ruled the Middle East and North Africa.

Egypt was also subject to foreign dominance: The Persians, Babylonians, Greeks, and Romans all conquered Egypt. The Ottoman Empire gained control of Egypt in 1517; the British in 1914; and finally, modern-day independence came in 1953.

The Evangelical Presbyterian Church is a tiny but strong presence for the gospel in Egypt, and many Coptic are sharing their faith as well. It has not been uncommon for Egyptian believers to be imprisoned for their faith, and despite the prevailing fear amongst Christians in Egypt, many are testifying to their faith in Christ. A unique Luis Palau evangelistic campaign was recently conducted in Egypt, where the meetings were videotaped at the central meeting place in Cairo and then copied and carried to over 600 locations the next night to be shown to eager viewers in halls, churches, and homes!

In the past, Egyptian tentmakers have gone all over North Africa and the Middle East to spread the gospel. As we lift up Egypt before the Lord, please ask God for the Spirit to awaken the church in Egypt to its responsibility and opportunity to take the gospel to Arabic brothers in more closed countries. May God raise up an army of Egyptians to carry the gospel to the nations!

## Prayer Points

- ⌣· There has often been conflict and disunity between believers in Egypt. Pray for the church to be one in Christ so that the world will know Jesus.
- ⌣· Intercede against fear that holds back many believers from speaking up about their faith in Christ.
- ⌣· One key pastor in Cairo and several Coptic priests have been very courageous in sharing their faith. Pray for these men to be protected, strengthened, and given a platform to influence the church.
- ⌣· Pray for the millions of poor living in the slums of Cairo to hear the good news, and for their suffering to be alleviated.
- ⌣· Ask God to break the powers of Islamic fundamentalism, especially at El Azhar University in Cairo. It is the largest Islamic university in the world and a center for training hundreds of Muslim missionaries who are sent out each year to spread Islam.

# Uzbekistan

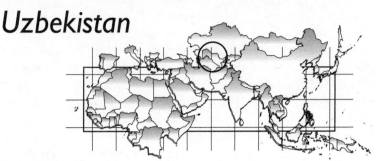

**Capital:** Tashkent
**Population:** 21,000,000
**Languages:** Uzbek, Russian
**Major Religions:** Islam, Russian Orthodoxy
**Major People Groups:** Uzbek, Russian, Tajik, Kazak, Tatar, Karakalpak
**Strategic Town or City:** Yangiyul

The church in Uzbekistan has grown rapidly since the country gained independence in 1991. This has happened despite intense opposition from Muslim clerics and government leaders. One Uzbek evangelist has started over 30 churches! This courageous man typically preaches boldly in small towns, with signs and wonders confirming his ministry.

Uzbekistan is the dominant political and economic force in Central Asia. The Uzbeks, descendants of Mongol warriors, once ruled all of Central Asia; but by the late 19th century, the region was subject to repeated Russian invasions. Once it became a republic of the USSR, the Soviets worked to dilute Uzbek national identity by flooding the nation with ethnic Russians, closing mosques, and persecuting Muslim leaders.

Since independence was declared, few changes have taken place in the government. The same "old guard" is in power, and they will take whatever steps they view necessary to insure their grip on power. This includes cracking down on both evangelical Christians and devout Muslims, both of whom are viewed as dangerous to political stability. There are over 5,000 mosques in Uzbekistan, so the government leaders are aware of the potential political force Islam has in the country.

Another enemy of the gospel in Uzbekistan is conflict within families, and a general hardness of heart that seems prevalent throughout Uzbekistan, especially in the villages.

As we join with believers worldwide to pray through the 10/40 Window, let us focus our prayers on holding back the forces of darkness that are intent on using government officials to oppose the purposes of God. Let us pray that Uzbekistan will fulfill its destiny in God to be a people who bless the other nations of Central Asia by being a missionary-sending nation!

## *Prayer Points*

- Pray for the president of Uzbekistan and other government leaders: Bless them, ask God to forgive them for persecuting the Uzbek believers, and ask the Father to reveal His great love to them.
- Intercede for the government leaders, that the blinders will fall off their eyes and that they will see the truth of the gospel. Pray for them to desire freedom of speech, freedom of religion, and freedom for their people to choose their own government leaders.
- Pray for the church to be strong during this time of persecution. Lift up the hands of those who are weary and about to give up.
- Let us ask our Father to use the persecution of His church to glorify Himself and to lead to the further spread of the gospel.
- Ask the Father to soften the hearts of village Uzbeks and bring whole families to Himself, using signs and wonders and the love of the people working there. Pray for encouragement

for Christian workers in villages who are often met with suspicion and malice.

⌣· In prayer, break the yoke of oppression in families. Ask our Father to teach fathers and mothers to love their children, husbands and wives to love each other, and children to love their parents and their siblings.

⌣· Pray for more workers to be raised up to go to Uzbekistan and for the spirit of fear over the land to be broken. Ask the Holy Spirit to raise up laborers from indigenous churches in the bordering nations of Kazakstan, Kyrgyzstan, Turkmenistan, and Afghanistan to reach Uzbeks for Christ!

# Nepal

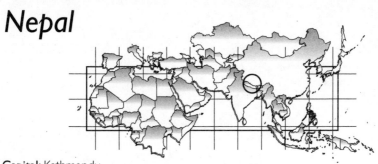

**Capital:** Kathmandu
**Population:** 24,300,000
**Languages:** Nepali, English, Sherpa
**Major Religions:** Hinduism, Christianity
**Major People Groups:** Nepali, Maithili, Bhojpuri, Sherpa
**Strategic Town or City:** Kathmandu

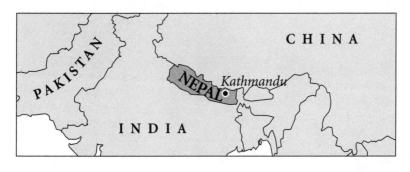

Nepal was a closed Hindu kingdom, cut off from the world for many centuries. Surrounded by the beautiful Himalayan Mountains, Nepal is a modern-day reminder of the Book of Acts. Starting with about 1,500 believers in 1970, the church doubled in size every year for many years. Today, there are over 250,000 believers! One village evangelist recently testified that he had over 100 converts to Christ from Hinduism in three months of preaching in the villages!

On Easter Sunday, 1991, an Easter sunrise service was held in downtown Kathmandu with over 15,000 believers in attendance. It is illegal to convert anyone from the religion of their ancestors, and for many years Hindu converts were put in prison for up to six years at a time. Persecution goes on in the villages, but the church is multiplying and seeing many come to Christ.

The Nepali people are deeply religious; they value modesty, spirituality, and are afraid of spirits. One of the greatest needs in the nation today is for unity between believers; in foreign countries, denominations are paying pastors to align themselves with their brand of Christianity, and this is causing division and mistrust among Christians.

## Prayer Points

⌣· Pray Jesus' prayer in John 17 over the nation of Nepal. Ask God to bring a spirit of repentance to the church, especially for competition between churches, pastors, and missionary organizations.

⌣· Lift up the church, that it will continue to multiply and grow. This is a season of great harvest in Nepal; many Hindus continue to come to Christ. May it not stop!

⌣· Pray for protection for the many new churches scattered across the country.

⌣· Ask the Father to bring a revival of holiness and hatred of sin.

⌣· Thank God for the many medical and community development workers in Nepal. Pray for their passion for evangelism to increase, even as they minister to the physical needs of people.

⌣· The government has tightened down on Christian workers: The homes of believers are being searched, threatening phone calls are being received, and visas are being denied. Ask the Holy Spirit to change the hearts of officials and the government in power so they see the blessing of having guest workers from other lands in Nepal.

# United Arab Emirates

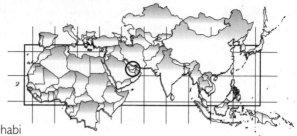

**Capital:** Abu Dhabi
**Population:** 2,000,000
**Languages:** Arabic, Persian
**Major Religion:** Islam
**Major People Groups:** Arab, Pakistani, Indian
**Strategic Town or City:** Dubayy

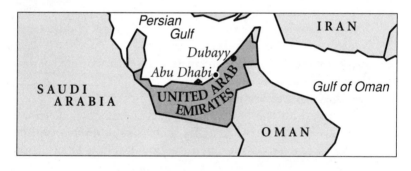

   The United Arab Emirates is a federation of seven states, or emirates, long ruled by tribal chiefs called sheiks or emirs. Once a center for piracy, this part of the Persian Gulf was known as the Pirate Coast. They became a British colony in the 19th century and remained under British protection until their independence in 1971.

   Sheik Zaid bin Sultan al-Nahayan of Abu Dhabi (the capital) has been president of the UAE since their independence. He has been a major force in maintaining the federation because of his dedication to a cooperative approach to development. Before oil was discovered in 1956, the people worked mostly within family structures as herdsman, traders, date farmers, or pearl divers. At one time, each tribe recognized the leader of their tribal group as the representative in disputes with other tribes; a strong sense of family and tribal loyalty still prevails.

The Christian church has enjoyed favor from the rulers, which is due, by and large, to how well Christian agencies have conducted themselves in their ministries and relationships. The tolerance for Christianity is an open door that is found in few places. Although evangelism of Muslims is prohibited, the UAE offers more opportunities for Christian workers than other Middle Eastern countries.

Some Muslims have accepted Christ, but most of them have emigrated rather than face severe repercussions from the government.

## Prayer Points

- Pray for the believers in the UAE to be filled with a spirit of boldness and zeal to share God's love with the lost people around them.
- Ask God to fill the expatriates with His Spirit and to give them faith and boldness to witness to Muslims.
- Thank our Lord for the favor the church has been given, but ask God that it will not turn into a trap, keeping the believers from taking risks, witnessing to their faith in Christ, and believing God for miracles and breakthroughs.
- Pray against the spirit of fear that comes over Christians working in Muslim lands.
- Intercede for the leaders of the UAE, especially that God will reveal Himself in dreams and visions. Ask the Lord to create spiritual hunger in their hearts for the gospel.

# Albania

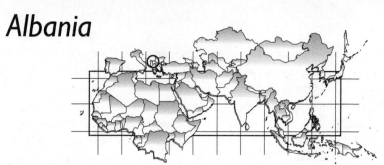

**Capital:** Tirana
**Population:** 3,800,000
**Language:** Tosk Albanian
**Major Religions:** Atheism, Islam
**Major People Groups:** Albanian, Gypsy, Greek
**Strategic Town or City:** Durres

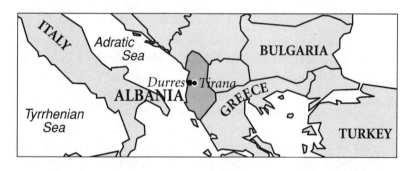

President Enver Hoxha once bragged that he had created the first totally atheist state in the world. Later, he was imprisoned, and at the time, Christians were preaching the gospel in the national football stadium! The first Christian book to be published openly in Albania, *The Father Heart of God,* was responsible for many Albanians coming to Christ.

Albania was under the grip of Communism from 1945 until 1991. During that time, the Communists severely persecuted members of all religions, driving Christians, Muslims, and others deeply underground. Dictator Enver Hoxha ruled with savagery and intimidation. Some 700,000 of his so-called "enemies" were killed or imprisoned during his rule. Neighbors were coerced into spying on neighbors.

The Communist regime left Albania in economic ruin. The nation is reeling under a 70% unemployment rate. Personal annual income is $250, and the economy survives only through black market smuggling and aid from Western nations. Albania now has a democratic form of government, but healing and recovery have been slow. Making matters more difficult is Albania's growing health crisis. AIDS, typhoid, and especially cholera are all spreading.

Muslims have mounted an aggressive campaign to re-Islamize Albania. Muslim missionaries, scholarships, monetary aid and mosque building have all risen dramatically since the fall of Communism. The Catholic and Orthodox churches are also reasserting their presence. There are currently some 32 evangelical Christian mission agencies working in Albania, and evangelicals are active in 22 of Albania's 32 districts. Although approximately 40% of the population is Muslim, many are open to hearing the good news of Christ. Many new churches have been planted in Albania, and there are incredible opportunities for those who are willing to go. It is not unusual for churches to be started through the efforts of short-term teams, which means there is a great need for follow-up and for long-term workers.

During the annual Islamic festival of Kurban, Muslims sacrifice goats and lambs to atone for their sins. One missionary reported, "Having lived in America for most of my life, I've never actually seen people sacrificing animals to their god for forgiveness of sins. As I walked down the streets, I saw at least 100–200 men carrying animals. This renewed my faith and reassured me that Jesus paid the final sacrifice for everyone." Praise the Lord for the atoning blood of Jesus!

## Prayer Points

- Thank the Lord for Christian books that have been translated and published in Albania. There is a tremendous response to Christian books and to the Word of God. Ask God to anoint His Word and other Christian literature so that it penetrates the hearts of those who read it.

⌣· Lift up the leaders of the many new churches planted in the last ten years. Ask God to equip and strengthen new leaders as they grow in their faith. May God protect them from economic pressure and the temptations they face.

⌣· Ask God to protect Christian workers and spiritual leaders from gangs, riots, and the chaos and violence throughout the country, especially in Tirana. He has opened blind eyes; may He also close seeing eyes so none of His children are harmed.

⌣· The economy has crashed, and many people are suffering. Ask God for mercy for Albania. Pray especially for the children, that they might not grow up bitter and hopeless.

⌣· Ask the Lord to hold back the influence of Islam and expose the plans of the enemy to bring destruction and chaos. May God reveal His Son, Jesus, to Albania!

# Morocco

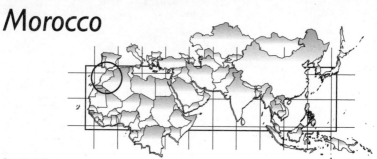

**Capital:** Rabat
**Population:** 31,600,000
**Languages:** Moroccan, Arabic, French, various Berber dialects
**Major Religion:** Islam
**Major People Groups:** Moroccan Arabs, various Berber groups, Southern Shilha, Riff, Central Shilha
**Strategic Town or City:** Casablanca

A tattoo of four distinct dots in the shape of a cross is found on the chin of every Berber woman, an ongoing reminder of their distant Christian past. Islam did not conquer Morocco with a sword as it did throughout the rest of North Africa. Instead, nominal Christianity welcomed it in the seventh century!

Scattered in a modern-day diaspora from Amsterdam to Paris, Berber people once ruled North Africa's mountains. In the 11th and 12th centuries, a Berber empire controlled all of northwest Africa and most of Spain. Berbers still play a significant part in Moroccan culture, although many have now been assimilated into the more dominant Arab population.

Though Islam in Morocco is not known to be militant in nature, there has always been resistance to change and foreign influence. Many of the religious practices in Morocco predate the advent of Islamic influence. A form of folk Islam dominates, led by the *marabouts*, holy men in every community who are consulted to solve problems, place curses, heal diseases, and cast out spirits. When a marabout dies, his grave may become a place of pilgrimage, visited by those seeking *baraka* (blessing), healing, or deliverance from evil spirits.

Although it is illegal to convert from Islam to Christianity in Morocco, a number of Moroccans have put their faith in Christ in the last 30 years. They face struggles due to persecution and ostracism, mostly from family and friends. Many have found Christ while visiting or living in the West.

Recently, an animated presentation of the gospel in parable form was shown on Dutch national television in a Berber language. This presentation, available on video, has been received with great curiosity and openness amongst the Berber people.

## *Prayer Points*

- Pray for the *Jesus* film, the animated gospel presentation, and gospel literature to get into the hands of those who are open and ready to hear the gospel.

- Join your prayers with others praying for Morocco for the seed of the gospel being broadcast on Christian radio in Arabic and Berber languages to be heard in Morocco, received, and protected. Pray for the ministry of satellite television, which can be received by many homes throughout Morocco that have satellite dishes. God promises us in the Scripture that His Word will not return void.

- Lift up those individuals and teams preparing to go to Morocco, and pray for believers who are serving the peoples of Morocco to be well-received and protected.

- Pray fervently for many more workers to be raised up to minister to Moroccan Arabs and Berbers in the great cities of Europe. There are already some working among them;

remember our brothers and sisters before the throne of God today, that they will be encouraged and see fruit for their labor. God is able!

- ⌣· Pray for authorities: the King of Morocco, Hassan II and his household; for government officials; the police; and Muslim leaders; that they will be instruments in the hand of God and that His salvation might be known among all the nations.

- ⌣· God loves all the peoples of Morocco. Stand in prayer for Christians laboring in Morocco, that their witness will be empowered by the Holy Spirit and that those open to receiving Jesus will overcome the spirit of fear and know God's strength in the face of any persecution.

# Iraq

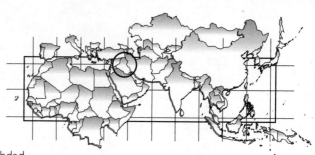

**Capital:** Baghdad
**Population:** 27,200,000
**Languages:** Arabic, Kurdish
**Major Religion:** Islam
**Major People Groups:** Arab, Kurd, Turkmen, Bedouin
**Strategic Town or City:** Al-Mawsil

On Christmas Eve, 1991, the *Jesus* film was shown in Iraq to a potential audience of over 17 million viewers! As a result, approximately 40 tons of Bibles were shipped into Iraq from Jordan to meet the demand for God's Word. In most people's minds, the image of Saddam Hussein's sinister glare and ruthless rule of Iraq does not fit with the freedom to show the *Jesus* film and distribute Bibles. But such are the ironies that make up this country.

There is an unusual amount of freedom for Iraqi believers; several churches in Baghdad meet openly to worship the Lord. A team visiting Iraq found much more openness to the gospel in Iraqis than in the people of other Muslim lands.

Iraq sits in the cradle of civilization. It has been the site of historic events since the beginning of time, including the Garden of Eden, the tower of Babel, and the call of Abraham. And though the world knows Iraq for the Gulf War, terrorists, and petroleum, Bible scholars know it as Nebuchadnezzar's Babylon.

One of the greatest challenges in praying for Iraq is for believers to repent of their prejudice against Saddam Hussein, so they can see him as an object of God's love and not just a terrorist and troublemaker. There is a tendency to stereotype Arabs and Muslims, rather than see them as God's creation and future co-workers in the gospel.

The long history of Iraq reminds us that, in God's patience and mercy, He has a plan to bless and redeem the Iraqi people. Life began in the rich land of the Tigris and Euphrates river deltas of Iraq, and the Persian and Babylonian empires have come and gone; but as the Book of Daniel reminds us, kingdoms come and kingdoms go, but God reigns forever! One government after another has ruled the Iraqi people in this expansive desert land, including the Mongols, the Ottomans, the Turks, and the British.

The Iraqi people received independence in 1945, but they, in turn, have oppressed another people, the Kurds. The Kurds are the largest people group in the world (around 25 million) who do not have their own country. Many of them live in Iraq, making up about 23% of the population of the country. The Kurds occupy the northern part of the country that borders Turkey, where three great civilizations come together: Arab, Persia, and Turkey. The Kurds long for a homeland of their own, but instead must live in a land where the leader practices genocide of their people.

Many Iraqis believe something must be wrong with their religion since their god was unable to help them win the Gulf War. They also believe the Gulf War was a demonstration of what the Bible writes about in the Book of Revelation, when the water flows with blood and smoke rises up from the weapons (see Revelation 11:6, 16:4, and chapter 18).

A decade of war and hardship has humbled the Iraqi people and led to a greater openness to change. Christian literature is in great demand in Iraq, and there is an increased respect for Christians. Pray for the people of Iraq, that they will see Jesus and believe that He is the Son of God.

## Prayer Points

- Pray for the Kurds, that God will alleviate their pain and suffering and that their hearts and minds will be open to the gospel.
- Lift up Saddam Hussein and those who lead the country with him. Ask the Lord to overrule any schemes Saddam Hussein might have for evil, and to turn his heart to the Lord Jesus. Might he see visions and dreams of the God of heaven just as Nebuchadnezzar did!
- Pray for believers to be bold and courageous in sharing their faith and standing up for their belief in Christ.
- Ask the Lord to remove the fear and prejudice in the hearts of Christians around the world, and for them to love the Iraqi people with God's love.
- Stand against the spiritual forces that want to use Saddam Hussein for war and destruction, and that the light of the gospel will penetrate the spiritual darkness over the land.
- Many Muslims are disillusioned with Islam; pray fervently that the veil over their eyes will be removed and they will see Jesus.

# Sri Lanka

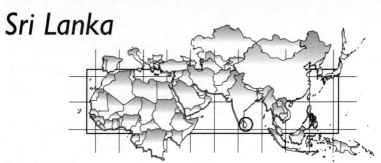

**Capital:** Colombo
**Population:** 19,400,000
**Languages:** English, Sinhala, Tamil
**Major Religions:** Buddhism, Hinduism, Islam, Christianity
**Major People Groups:** Sinhalese, Tamil
**Strategic Town or City:** Dehiwala–Mount Lavinia

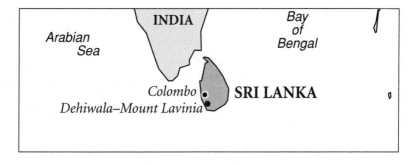

Ceylon, as it was known for many years, has been embroiled in a civil war for almost 25 years. This tiny island nation that once was famous for its friendly people and tea plantations, is now in the news because of car bombings and fighting between the Hindu Tamil and the Buddhist Sinhalese. Sri Lanka received its independence from Great Britain in 1948.

Sri Lanka is one of the few Buddhist nations in the world, idealizing self-purification and denial of all desire in order to attain nirvana, or perfect bliss. Sri Lanka's Buddhists, who make up the predominant Sinhalese population, try to convert anyone who believes differently than they. Discrimination against Hindus and Christians is common.

Sri Lanka has been a sending base for Buddhist missionaries for hundreds of years. Although the Christian church is well established in Sri Lanka, its influence has steadily declined due to nominal Christianity and the emigration of Christians. That trend has been reversed in the last few years, with a strong influence coming through indigenous church planters and parachurch organizations.

## Prayer Points

⌣· Pray for the church to be reawakened and purified so that its witness to Christ will be faithful, courageous, and pure.

⌣· Ask the Lord of the Harvest to raise up more missionaries who will be willing to serve in a war-torn environment.

⌣· Pray for a resurgence of evangelistic fervor born out of a devotion to the worship of Jesus in the nations. Ask the Lord to strengthen the church in doctrinal purity and for the truths they believe to become fervent in their hearts.

⌣· Lift up those Sri Lankans who are serving the Lord faithfully; pray for protection, encouragement, and wisdom.

⌣· Pray against the spirit of violence and bitterness in the hearts of the people affected by the fighting. Many families have lost sons in the conflict. Ask God for peace to rule in Sri Lanka, so that He will be glorified and the hearts of the people will be open to the gospel.

# Israel and Gaza

**Capital:** Jerusalem
**Population:** 6,163,000 in Israel, and another 975,000 people in Gaza
**Major Languages:** Hebrew, Arabic, English
**Major Religions:** Judaism and Islam
**Major People Groups:** Jewish, Arabic, Palestinian
**Strategic Town or City:** Tel Aviv

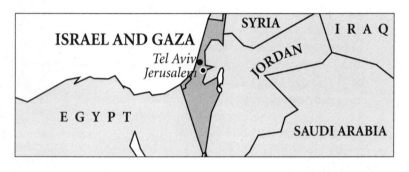

The modern nation of Israel is home to three of the world's great religions: Islam, Christianity, and Judaism. In 1947, the United Nations voted to divide the area, then known as Palestine, into Jewish and Arab states, although Arabs rejected this partition.

Following the partition, many Palestinians and Arabs lost their homes and land to Jewish settlers, sometimes to neighbors they had lived beside for years. Since that time, the Palestinians have been without a home and have been manipulated by international politics. Millions live in refugee camps in the surrounding Arab countries, with little or no hope of returning to their former homeland.

The present peace process needs our prayers and support; the destiny of millions of people rides on the outcome. The peace talks did produce a historic agreement between Israel and the Palestine Liberation Organization (PLO) in September of 1993. The PLO recognized the right of Israel to exist, and Israel recognized the PLO as the representative of the Palestinian people. Limited self-rule was granted to the PLO in Gaza and the West Bank, beginning with the city of Jericho. Although repeatedly challenged by extremist groups on both sides, the peace process is still in motion and holding firm.

Christianity's historical mistreatment of Jews and Arabs has hindered the furtherance of the gospel in Israel and has raised significant barriers to keep Jews and Arabs from coming to Christ. Both Jews and Muslims consider conversion to Christ unpatriotic. The devastating effect of the medieval Crusades continues to this day.

There are many indigenous believers in Israel, both Arabs and Jews. However, the number of Palestinian and Arab believers is much higher, numbering in the hundreds of thousands.

## Prayer Points

- Lift up the Christians of all races in Israel. Pray for unity among them. Pray for hurts, suspicions, and mistrust to be broken down between them. Ask God to give the believers discernment into the political manipulation of their leaders, so they will see each other through the eyes of Christ and not through political lenses.
- Pray for the spread of the gospel and for many churches to be planted throughout the country.
- Ask God for peace in Israel. No one wins when there is war and killing.
- God made all the peoples of the earth (Acts 17:24–26). Intercede for the Palestinians to have a land of their own. God created them and loves them—may the Palestinians know this to be true firsthand.
- Pray for Jesus Christ, the Messiah, to be revealed to the Jewish people in Israel!

# Tajikistan

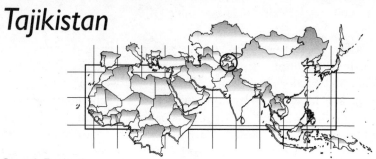

**Capital:** Dushanbe
**Population:** 5,300,000
**Languages:** Tajik, Russian
**Major Religions:** Islam, Russian Orthodox Christianity
**Major People Groups:** Tajik, Uzbek, Russian
**Strategic Town or City:** Khojend

The Tajik people are Persian and speak a Persian dialect, in contrast to the other large people groups of Central Asia, which are Turkic in origin. The Tajik are found throughout Central Asia and in especially large numbers in Afghanistan and Uzbekistan.

Islam came to Tajikistan in the seventh century. Since the middle of the 1800s the Russians dominated the region; the Tajik Republic was formed in 1991 from areas that were populated primarily by the Tajik people.

Tajikistan is a very poor country with an economy heavily dependent on cotton. The most traditional Tajik live in the mountains that cover most of the country. Since independence in 1991, Tajikistan has been influenced by Shiite fundamentalism due to its close ethnic ties with Iran. Many new mosques have been built. Very few Christian workers have gained access to this tiny nation, but it has not been forgotten. Several Christian groups are targeting the Tajik people in prayer and have plans to send long-term teams. There is a spiritual hunger in the hearts of young Tajik, and they deeply desire to discover their cultural and ethnic roots.

Life in Tajikistan has been marked by ongoing clan and civil warfare, spilling over into Uzbekistan and Afghanistan. This makes living conditions difficult but certainly not impossible. It is time to focus prayer on this little-known but not forgotten country. Our prayers could be the spiritual turning point in the history of Tajikistan!

## Prayer Points

- Pray for openness to the gospel; ask God for the conditions necessary to create a spiritual hunger for the gospel in the hearts of the people.
- The Tajik people have been oppressed by other nations; pray that in their search for identity, they will find it in Jesus!
- Pray for freedom in this nation and that the government leaders would be more open to the assistance of foreign workers and nongovernment agencies in economic development.
- Pray against the influence of Shiite fundamentalism from Iran.
- Ask the Holy Spirit to raise up many more laborers to carry the message of the gospel to the Tajik people, and that Tajik evangelists, pastors, and church planters will be raised up to reach their own people.
- Pray for doors to open up to take the gospel to remote mountain villages.

# China

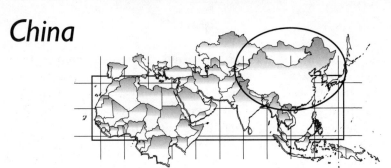

**Capital:** Beijing
**Population:** 1,280,000,000
**Languages:** Mandarin, Cantonese, and many more
**Major Religions:** Christianity, Taoism, Buddhism, Confucianism, animism, Islam
**Major People Groups:** Han Chinese, 55 official ethnic minorities
**Strategic Town or City:** Shanghai

One of the greatest revivals, if not the greatest, in the history of the church has taken place in China in the last 50 years. Approximately 1,200 people come to Christ every hour in this vast and divergent land. All 27 provinces have been touched by the gospel.

About one in five people on the planet are Chinese, and more than 30 million Chinese live in other countries. China is home to many unreached people groups, including the Zhuang, Uygur, and Hui.

A Chinese girl from Hong Kong was recently in China on an outreach to the Zhuang people. She witnessed to an older man squatting in front of his one-room home in a Zhuang village. As she shared about the gospel with the old grandfather, she couldn't help but notice the differences between them: age, clothing, gender, material prosperity—everything about their lives was different. Yet there was one thing they had in common: They were both hungry for the truth. The humble, old gentleman accepted Christ as his personal Savior that day, and a Chinese teenager experienced the reality of God using her to spread the worship of Jesus to the unreached.

Months later the man wrote to the teenage girl and invited her back to his village to share the gospel with his family. When she arrived, over 70 family members were respectfully waiting to hear the message that had changed their grandfather's life. All of them accepted Christ. Today, there is a thriving church of over 1,000 believers in that village; Grandfather and the other elders in the congregation are now training the young people to go as village workers to other towns and cities to share the good news. Several daughter churches have been started.

God is moving in China. Centuries of superstition and animism are being swept aside by the wind of the Spirit. The move of God in China is one more example of what God is doing to spread His glory to the nations. The Spirit of the living God is moving on the face of the whole earth. Today, let us celebrate and thank God for what He is doing in China.

## *Prayer Points*

- Pray for the Chinese church to get a vision for spreading the gospel to other peoples and lands. Chinese believers most often go to other Chinese when they reach out in evangelism. The Body of Christ around the world desperately needs our Chinese brothers and sisters, especially the lessons they have learned from years of persecution and suffering. May God raise up an army of Chinese missionaries to sweep over the earth!
- Pray for the unreached people groups of China. Ask the Father to move on the hearts of the church leaders in China and tear down the walls of fear, prejudice, and ethnocentrism

so that He may use the Han Chinese to reach many other peoples with the good news.

~· There is still persecution in China. Lift up our brothers and sisters before the throne of God. Ask the Lord to move on the hearts of Chinese officials to lift the persecution and see the church favorably. Also, intercede that they will release all believers who are in prison for their faith, and until that is done, that the saints will be strengthened with great courage and faith.

# Djibouti

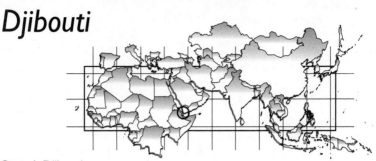

**Capital:** Djibouti
**Population:** 523,000
**Languages:** French, Arabic, Afar, Somali
**Major Religions:** Islam and Roman Catholicism
**Major People Groups:** Issa, Somali, Afar, Arab
**Strategic Town or City:** Djibouti

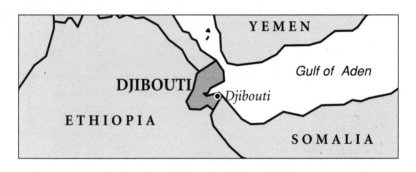

The tiny nation of Djibouti, located on the horn of Africa, is known to be the hottest country in the world, as well as one of the poorest. Djibouti was France's last colony in Africa. At the time of its independence in 1977, Djibouti had only three college graduates and little skilled labor. Its only resources were sand, salt, and its strategic location.

The people groups in Djibouti are loyal Muslims, with strong ties to Saudi Arabia. However, there is a small, struggling church in Djibouti composed primarily of ethnic Somalis.

Djibouti's political instability contributes to its suspicion of visitors in general and Westerners in particular. There is tension between the Afars and Issas, and although all prime ministers since independence have been Afars, there are allegations that the Issas dominate the country. This has resulted in large-scale Afar insurgency in the northern part of the country.

Little is known about the believers in Djibouti, but it is clear that God's Word calls us to remember those who suffer for their faith. Today is a day in which the church around the world will remember our brothers and sisters in that faraway land. Let us remember them with fervent, compassionate prayers and with faith in our hearts that our prayers will affect the course of history in Djibouti.

## Prayer Points

⌣· Pray for the church to be strengthened and encouraged.
⌣· Ask God to bring many more believers into His church in Djibouti, and that the fighting between the Afars and the Issas will lead to greater openness to the gospel.
⌣· Intercede for African laborers from other countries to be called to Djibouti.
⌣· Let us believe the Lord for His church to be planted among the Afars and Issas.
⌣· Ask God to give the believers keys to bless the land economically. May His church be a channel of prosperity and healing in the land.
⌣· Pray for peace in Djibouti and for the forces of darkness to be hindered in their plans to use Djibouti to stir up war and strife.

# Yemen

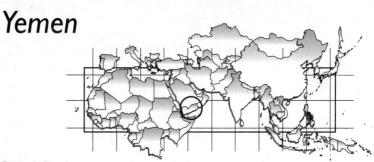

**Capital:** Sana'a
**Population:** 13,600,000
**Language:** Arabic
**Major Religion:** Islam
**Major People Group:** Yemeni Arab
**Strategic Town or City:** Adan

Yemen is one of the oldest inhabited areas of the world. Sana'a, the northern capital, is considered to be the city Shem settled after the flood.

The Bible refers to Yemen's gold, spices, and precious stones as gifts to King Solomon from the Queen of Sheba when she came to learn about the God who blessed Israel. There was a strong Christian influence in Yemen from the third to the fifth century, but when Islam arose in the fifth century, Yemen was one of the first countries to follow the prophet Mohammed. It is home to two of the oldest mosques in the world.

Today, Yemen is a political flashpoint, divided by Marxism (South Yemen, formed in 1967, became the only Arab Marxist state in the world), economic depression, and massive underde-velopment. In 1990, economic pressures forced North and South Yemen to unite, but the union between the two remains tense. Yemen has no rich oil deposits like Saudi Arabia or the other Persian Gulf States to provide a ready source of wealth. Most Yemenis depend on money earned by relatives working in other countries. After the Gulf War, in which Yemen sided with Iraq, Yemenis in Saudi Arabia were expelled, exacerbating the eco-nomic crisis at home.

Most Yemenis live in villages or on small farms. Yemenis trace their history and traditions through songs and poems. The Socotri, Mahri, and Bedouin people groups in Yemen are totally unreached with the gospel.

However, there are opportunities for Westerners visiting the cities, even for just a week or so. One short-term team found amazing opportunities to witness to women in the restaurants. One young woman had entered a restaurant in typical Yemeni costume, fully veiled and wearing a long black dress. But when she encountered the American team of Christian "tourists," in the back section where women could remove their veils, she underwent a sudden transformation. Discarding her veil and robes, she emerged in lipstick, jeans, and a T-shirt, then added the baseball cap of one of the team members, donning it backward for a thoroughly Western effect. With a lit cigarette in her lips, she couldn't have looked less Muslim, and she listened with interest as they shared their faith. The team returned home convinced of the effectiveness of restaurant evangelism as a strategy!

Let us pray today that Yemen, like the Queen of Sheba in days of old, will seek the God who blesses His people with redemption, and that workers will go in with creative and effec-tive strategies to share the good news!

## Prayer Points

⌣· Yemenis regularly hear the gospel on Christian radio broad-casts. Pray that this will lead to churches being planted and believers being equipped to share the gospel with others.

- Stand in the place of intercession for the Yemeni believers, who are alone and face great pressure and persecution from families, friends, and the state. Pray that they will be strong and that their faith will fail not.
- Pray for the peace of Yemen. Ask God to touch the hearts of those who exploit the poverty of the people for their own political gain.
- Pray for laborers! The need is great, and the people are desperate for help.
- Believe God that doors will open for missionaries, medical workers, and church planters. Pray that as they respond to the opportunities, they will be bold and passionate in their zeal for the lost and the glory of God.
- Yemen holds a strategic location geographically; ask God to protect it from radical elements that want to use it to create political hegemony and further their own causes.

# Vietnam

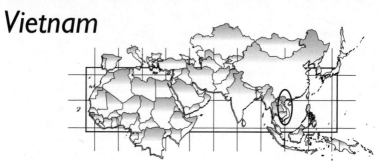

**Capital:** Hanoi
**Population:** 88,300,000
**Languages:** Vietnamese, French, Chinese
**Major Religions:** Buddhism, Roman Catholicism
**Major People Groups:** Vietnamese, Khmer, Hmong, Muong, Tho, Miao
**Strategic Town or City:** Ho Chi Minh

Vietnam's beautiful countryside of rice paddies, mountains, and rural villages stretches for over 1,000 miles along the South China Sea. But Vietnam has not always experienced serene beauty; war has marred the landscape and foreign powers have ruthlessly dominated Vietnam for over 1,000 years.

First China, then France, and finally the United States sent their young men to fight and die in the steamy jungles and mountain passes of this rugged land. Vietnam's independence came when Communist guerillas under the leadership of Ho Chi Minh finally wrested control of both the northern and southern halves of the country.

The Buddhist religion practiced by the majority of the Vietnamese people is a blend of Confucianism, Taoism, and

Buddhism, with popular Chinese beliefs and ancient Vietnamese animism mixed in. This mixture of ancestor and spirit worship is known as Tam Giao. Though the gospel has been widely proclaimed in Vietnam, the hill tribes are isolated from these efforts to proclaim the good news. These groups include the Thai-Dai and Miao-Yao, as well as the Hung, May, and Nguon peoples.

It was not until the early part of 20th century that Protestant missionaries gained a permanent foothold in Vietnam, and even then the work was conducted largely by one mission, the Christian and Missionary Alliance. From the outset, those serving in Vietnam have suffered persecution. Though the nationals were normally open to the gospel, it was the ruling powers that felt threatened. During the French colonial period, evangelistic work was severely curtailed, and when the Japanese moved in during World War II, the missionaries who refused to leave were rounded up and held in internment camps.

It is said that the church is born in the blood of the martyrs, and that is certainly true of Vietnam. Playing the role of missionary heroine and martyr did not seem to fit the image of Betty Olsen. Yet in the early hours of the Tet offensive in 1968, she risked her life as she nursed the wounds of others around her. Betty, a self-possessed redhead, was thirty-four years old when she was taken captive by Vietcong guerillas. After eight months of walking 12 to 14 hours a day, and enduring mental and physical torture beyond description, Betty Olsen died. She suffered malnutrition, dysentery, her teeth were loose with bleeding gums, her hair was falling out from having nothing to eat but a meager portion of rice gruel each day, and leeches covered her legs.

At the end, she pleaded with her captors to let her die where she fell on the trail. Instead, she was beaten and forced to march on. Her final days defy description. A fellow captive, Mike Benge, an American AID officer, reports: "...she became so weak, she could not get out of her own hammock...." Her thirty-fifth birthday found her moaning in pain, lying filthy in her hammock. Two days later she passed on to be with Jesus. Later, Mike Benge told how he put his trust in God because of the witness of Betty Olsen.

Mike Benge reported that Betty hid her own meager rations to share with captured native Christians who had even less. In Betty, Mike found "the most unselfish person I have ever known." Her Christlike love was more than he could comprehend. "She never showed any bitterness or resentment. To the end she loved the ones who mistreated her." After spending five more years in captivity, Mike Benge was released to tell the world the story of Betty Olsen. Let us beseech the God of heaven to raise up many more like Betty Olsen, to lay down their lives that every man and woman, boy and girl will know that Jesus loves them.

## *Prayer Points*

- Ask the Holy Spirit to raise up a vast army of workers to go to Vietnam.
- Pray for the healing of the land and its people after so many years of fighting and warfare. Communism is one more form of oppression; ask God to liberate the people from this last vestige of foreign domination.
- Intercede for spiritual awakening among all those who profess the name of Jesus in Vietnam. Pray for revival to sweep the land!
- As believers gather each Sunday to worship, ask our Father in heaven to strengthen them, give them boldness, and take away fear and hurt. Ask the Lord to give the church leaders of Vietnam a burden to reach the hill tribes with the gospel and to dare to dream of sending missionaries to other lands!

# Taiwan

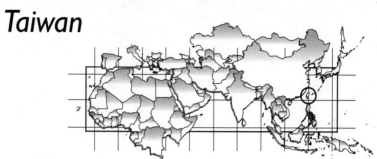

**Capital:** Taipei
**Population:** 22,100,000
**Languages:** Mandarin, Taiwanese, English, Hakka
**Major Religions:** Buddhism, Taoism, Confucianism, Christianity
**Major People Groups:** Han Chinese, Taiwanese, Hakka
**Strategic Town or City:** Kaohsiung

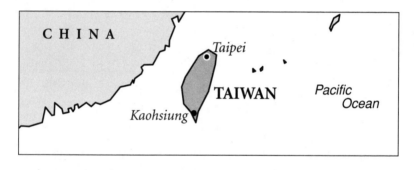

Although there are many churches in the large cities of Taiwan, traditional Chinese religions still shape the culture. Confucianism dictates social patterns and relationships, and Buddhism provides most rituals and beliefs. The Taiwanese burn incense and pray to their ancestors in Buddhist temples throughout the island nation. They believe that by doing this they can ward off evil spirits, hexes, and misfortune.

Many churches in Taiwan have grown stagnant and are in deep need of revival. Materialism and financial prosperity are false gods that have won the devotion of many of the people.

Taiwan, once called Formosa, was under Japanese control for the first half of the century. After World War II, members of the

Nationalist Chinese government, which still claims to represent all of China, fled to Taiwan from the mainland. Since that time, the government of Taiwan has been comprised mostly of mainlanders, but in recent years there has been a growing number of indigenous Taiwanese represented in the ruling party.

Taiwan faces the threat of war with mainland China and has become more and more isolated from the rest of the world as a result of economic and political pressure from mainland China.

## *Prayer Points*

⌣· Taiwan has the potential to be a great sending nation. Ask God to pour out His Spirit upon the church in Taiwan, and that He will move upon the church to evangelize the indigenous peoples of the island and send thousands of missionaries to the unreached.

⌣· Cry out to the Lord for revival in Taiwan. May He remove theological barriers, and may the fresh wind of His Spirit blow across the land.

⌣· Intercede for those planting churches among the aboriginal peoples and for Scripture to be translated into their own languages.

⌣· Ask the Lord of the Harvest to raise up missionaries from Africa and Latin America to serve in Taiwan. The doors are open for missionaries in church planting and many other avenues of service.

⌣· Believe God for a special blessing for missionaries studying Chinese, that they will have faith, discipline, and determination to be able to learn the language.

# Bahrain

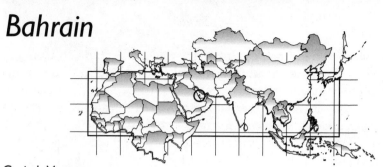

**Capital:** Manama
**Population:** 700,000
**Languages:** Arabic, English, Farsi, Urdu
**Major Religions:** Islam, Hinduism
**Major People Groups:** Arab, Indian, Pakistani, Iranian
**Strategic Town or City:** Al-Muharraq

The tiny island nation of Bahrain is made up of 35 sun-drenched islands situated between two Islamic superpowers. Bahrain gained independence from Great Britain in 1971 and is now ruled by a benevolent monarch. Although tiny in size, oil has made Bahrain a wealthy country and strategically important. In recent years, Bahrain has become a banking center in the Middle East as government leaders have attempted to diversify the nation's economy to shed its dependence on oil production.

Iran ruled the 35 islands that make up Bahrain for almost 200 years until the Kalifa family, an Arab dynasty from Arabia, took control in 1782. The same family controls Bahrain today. Bahrain has freedom of speech, press, and religion, although some human rights abuses remain. While evangelism is prohibited, Christian expatriates have found relative freedom and a warm welcome in Bahrain.

Bahrain is the playground of Muslim tourists in the Middle East. The relative openness of Bahrain provides a natural launching pad for initiatives for outreach throughout the Middle East.

## Prayer Points

- Pray that misconceptions about the gospel will be removed from the hearts and minds of the people of Bahrain.
- Thank God for the freedom that exists in Bahrain, and pray that the Holy Spirit will use it to penetrate the hearts of Arab visitors from other countries.
- Intercede for a move of God so great that unbelievers will cry out for God. Ask God for signs and wonders, for miracles that lead to pulling down the strongholds of deception and unbelief.
- Pray against a pleasure spirit that rules the hearts of many, and for there to be deep conviction of sin.
- Lift up Bahraini believers to be protected, strengthened, and fearless in their love of Jesus. Pray for them to have a fresh revelation of Jesus.

# Brunei

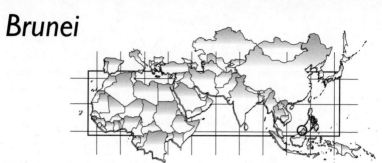

**Capital:** Bandar Seri Begawan
**Population:** 300,000
**Languages:** Malay, English, Chinese, Iban
**Major Religions:** Islam, Chinese Religions, Christianity
**Major People Groups:** Malay, Chinese, Iban
**Strategic Town or City:** Seria

The sultan of Brunei is the richest man in the world. He rules Brunei with an iron fist and fiercely guards his status as both political and spiritual leader of his people and their religious affiliation as Muslims.

Christianity is seen as threat, and the only Malay believers in the sultanate must meet secretly in caves and jungles. The rest of the believers are Chinese. Though the Chinese believers have limited freedom to congregate, the Malay believers do not enjoy that same liberty.

The British ruled Brunei for over 100 years until independence in 1984. English and Malay are the official languages of Brunei. Oil wealth makes it possible for the sultan to cover the costs of education and healthcare, which are free for every citizen.

Brunei turned to Islam in the 15th century through the conversion of Sultan Awang Alak Beter. He was a pagan ruler until he heard about Islam, probably through Muslim traders. To show his sincerity as a Muslim, he changed his name to Sultan Mohammed. Today's sultan is the 29th in his line.

Though tiny in geographical size, Brunei is a challenge to us to believe God that men and women from every tribe will worship the Lamb. Let us take hold of God's passion for His glory to be revealed through the worship of His Son in every place and by every people.

## Prayer Points

- Intercede for open doors for those whom God has called to go as missionaries to Brunei.
- Pray especially for Chinese believers who live in Brunei, or who can get into Brunei through family members or relatives, to be stirred with unusual faith for God to touch the heart of the sultan and the Malay people.
- Lift up the tribal peoples of the tiny nation; ask God to sovereignly penetrate the Iban people group.
- Focus your prayers on the sultan; may he humble himself and cry out to God for forgiveness and salvation. Ask God to reveal Himself to the sultan in dreams and visions.
- Pray for boldness among believers and a revelation of the reality of heaven and hell. Ask the Lord to stir their hearts with zeal for those who have not heard the good news.

# Lebanon

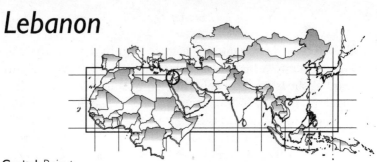

**Capital:** Beirut
**Population:** 4,100,000
**Languages:** Arabic, French
**Major Religions:** Islam, Roman Catholicism, Orthodox Christianity, Druze
**Major People Groups:** Lebanese, Syrian, Palestinian Arab
**Strategic Town or City:** Tarabulus

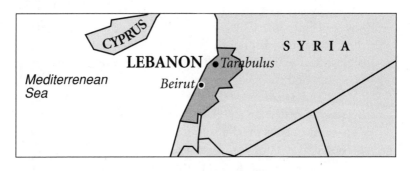

Lebanon has been wracked with war and civil war for decades. Only in recent years has this once beautiful Mediterranean country begun to recover. Once a playground for wealthy Muslims from all over the Middle East, it became instead a center for terrorists who kidnapped Westerners and held them for years for notoriety and financial gain. One third of the entire population has died or been lost to emigration since 1975.

Lebanon, the site of ancient Phoenicia, is a fertile coastal land, with beautiful mountains and lovely beaches. Beirut once boasted being one of the most beautiful cities in the world; today, it lies in shambles as a result of the fighting. Recovery began in 1992 when a new government was installed, but it will take years before Lebanon regains even part of its former glory.

At one time, Beirut was the headquarters for Christian efforts to evangelize Muslims in the Middle East. Christian organizations had to move their headquarters to Cyprus or London, but in spite of this setback, many Muslims have come to Christ in recent years. Lebanon is the only country in the Middle East besides Israel that does not have Islam as its state religion.

There are 17 official religious communities in Lebanon: one Jewish, five Muslim, and eleven Christian. Political fragmentation in the Christian community and intense personal rivalries have hindered reconciliation between these communities and prevented Lebanon from finding permanent solutions to the fighting.

The decline in residential missionaries, the emigration of national church leaders during the war, and a lack of trained Christian workers have left many congregations without pastoral care. There is a great need for workers who will brave the adverse conditions to live and work among the believers in Lebanon. Further, there are tremendous opportunities to share the gospel and to plant churches amongst Muslims. Syrian secret police operate freely, but in spite of persecution, the gospel is advancing. God has used the tragedies of war to create hunger in the hearts of many Lebanese people.

## Prayer Points

- War and hatred are platforms for the enemy to bring destruction and chaos. Pray against the hatred and rivalries that divide the people and give Satan entrance into the country.
- Pray for the believers to be covered with God's love and for angels to watch over them. Pray that God will protect them from the spirit of religious rivalry that divides the land.
- Ask the Lord to raise up workers to lay down their lives for Christ in Lebanon. The opportunities are great, but the risks are great as well.
- Stand with those who have converted from Islam and are in great need of fellowship, wisdom, and protection.
- Intercede that spiritual hunger and a quest for the truth will invade the hearts and minds of the unconverted and that many Muslims will come to Christ.
- Pray against fear!

# Qatar

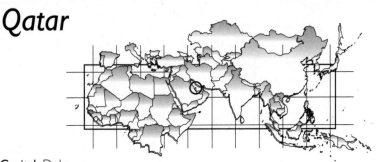

**Capital:** Doha
**Population:** 575,000
**Languages:** Arabic, English
**Major Religion:** Islam
**Major People Group:** Qatari Arab
**Strategic Town or City:** Ar-Rayyan

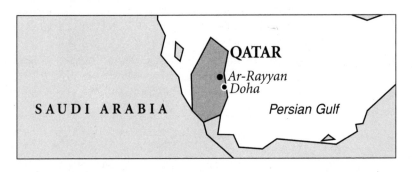

Qatar is located on the eastern coast of the Arabian Peninsula. The harsh, gravelly desert of this region is one of the harshest and least inhabited places on earth. Bedouin nomads settled in the Qatar peninsula in the 18th century and survived by fishing and diving for pearls.

Qatar was considered an insignificant backwater country until oil was discovered in 1932. Many Qataris saw the discovery as compensation from Allah for the harshness of their lives. Now the native Qataris, numbering about 110,000, are one the wealthiest people groups on the earth. Their welfare system is one of the most comprehensive in the world, including free education, free healthcare, free electricity, and free housing!

Expatriate Christians are allowed to meet together for worship. However, the Qataris are members of the Wahhabi, a reform movement that is committed to keeping Islam pure from outside influences, especially those associated with the oil industry.

The current ruling emir still runs the country much like a medieval sheikdom, with no elected posts and no voting rights. The emir rules by forging consensus among the male leadership of his family. Once chosen, the emir must continue to maintain positive consensus, not only by capably ruling the country, but also by encouraging good family relations.

## Prayer Points

⌣· Let us believe God to reveal Himself to the emir of Qatar, and to his fellow male family members who share with him in the ruling responsibilities. May God grant these men dreams and visions to create hunger in their hearts for God.

⌣· May God give the expatriate believers favor with the native Qataris, granting them boldness and supernatural anointing to share the gospel.

⌣· Pray that the Qataris' desire for purity, reflected in the Wahhabi sect's beliefs and practices, will lead them to honestly search for the truth.

⌣· Pray for signs and wonders to be done in the midst of the Qataris to confirm the truth that Jesus is the Son of God.

⌣· Ask the Lord to pull down the strongholds of fear, unbelief, and spiritual blindness that cover the eyes of the people.

⌣· Thank the Lord that He died for the Qataris, and ask God to move by His Spirit mightily in Qatar. Nothing is too hard for God!

# Turkmenistan

**Capital:** Ashkabad
**Population:** 3,700,000
**Languages:** Turkmen, Russian, Uzbek
**Major Religion:** Islam
**Major People Groups:** Turkmen, Russian, Kazak, Uzbek
**Strategic Town or City:** Chardzhou

Turkmenistan is an extremely poor country, dominated by an underdeveloped economy and a dictatorial leader. The Turkmen are traditionally a nomadic people who are at home in the harsh conditions of the Kara-Kum Desert. Geographic isolation has helped preserve the Turkmen culture.

Though the Turkmen resisted Russian domination, they were annexed by the tsars in 1885, and became a Soviet republic after the Bolshevik revolution. Turkmenistan is rich in natural resources, including petroleum and natural gas.

Turkmen are a hardy people, but have been dominated by Islam for many centuries. Most Turkmen practice a form of folk Islam, combining superstition, animism, and traditional beliefs.

Turkmenistan has retained the old Soviet-style secret police, and the few believers there are watched carefully. Workers in nongovernment agencies have freedom on a personal level to share the gospel, and there is openness to hear about the Lord Jesus. Today there are about 500 Turkmen believers.

Several months ago, a group of national Christians went into a rural village to show the *Jesus* film. The Turkmen showed up as whole families, the fathers in Western clothes, but the mothers wearing their long, colorful dresses and headscarves. These people had never heard the gospel before, and the showing of a film was a rather exciting event! Even more exciting was the harvest of this one visit; over 50 people put their faith in Christ, and their eternal destiny was changed forever!

There is a growing desire on the part of Turkmen believers to reach their own people in Afghanistan and Iran. There are several million Turkmen living outside Turkmenistan.

## Prayer Points

- Doors are open for nongovernment agencies to serve the people of Turkmenistan. Because of extreme poverty, Christians can have an impact on the nation and can help alleviate the suffering of the people. Pray that many more workers will go to Turkmenistan.
- Lift up the growing but still very small Turkmen church, especially for courage and faith. Ask the Father to raise up strong indigenous leaders to spread the gospel and shepherd the flock.
- Pray for God to close the eyes of Iranian secret police so the gospel can be spread to Turkmen in Iran. Ask for protection for Turkmen evangelists who are reaching their ethnic brothers with the good news.
- Pray for the president of Turkmenistan and for other government leaders that they will be open to Christians working in their nation. Let us join our faith and our prayers that many of them will come to Christ!
- Pray that the Turkmen Bible would be finished soon and would bring many more people to a knowledge of Christ.

# Ethiopia

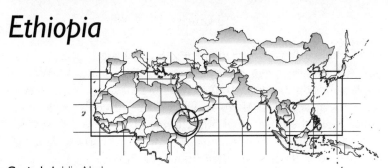

**Capital:** Addis Ababa
**Population:** 66,200,000
**Languages:** Amharic, Tigrinya, Orominga
**Major Religions:** Eastern Orthodox, Christianity, Islam, Protestant Christianity
**Major People Groups:** Amhara, Wellega, Tigrinya, Somali, Gurage
**Strategic Town or City:** Dire Dawa

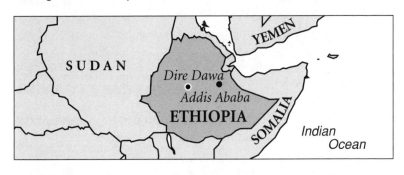

Ethiopia has a rich Christian tradition and is mentioned more than sixty times in the Bible. The rise of Islam in the seventh century led to conflict with the Coptic Church, already well established in Ethiopia. In spite of a warm response to the gospel through the centuries, millions of modern-day Ethiopians are still without the Christian message.

In 1928, Dr. Thomas Lambie opened up the southern provinces of Ethiopia to the gospel. He settled in the province of Wallamo, where he practiced medicine and conducted evangelistic work. Other missionaries joined him, and by the time they were forced out by the advancing forces of the Italian army prior to WWII, there was a small handful of 48 Wallamo believers. The missionaries left with a deep sense of sadness and doubt as to the fate of the new church. Would these young Christians be able to stand under the persecution that was sure to come?

Persecution did come—severe testing, including beatings and imprisonment—which led to rapid growth of the church. By 1941, the fighting in Ethiopia was over, and the following year the first missionaries were allowed to return. What they found was a great miracle: The 48 believers they had left had grown to over 10,000, in more than 100 congregations!

A series of droughts in the 1970s and 1980s killed tens of thousands of people, leaving the Ethiopian countryside barren and the people impoverished. When Ethiopia turned to Marxism, the nation was further devastated, only to be compounded by still more fighting with Eritrea.

Through all these difficulties, the church of Jesus Christ in Ethiopia has continued to grow and flourish. Let us remember our brothers and sisters in Ethiopia with fervent prayers on their behalf. Let us especially pray for the church in Ethiopia to reach out to those people groups within the borders of their land without the gospel. More than eighty languages are spoken in Ethiopia. Many of these groups are without the good news of God's love.

## Prayer Points

- Pray for peace in Ethiopia. Ask God to give stability in the government.
- Ethiopia is one of the poorest nations in the world. Ask the Lord to move on the hearts of His people worldwide to help create job schemes and to provide solutions for the vexing problems created by drought and famine.
- Ask God for unity among believers. The churches are often badly divided in Ethiopia, and this gives more ground for Islam to grow.
- Intercede for the strengthening of church leaders in the villages.

# Myanmar

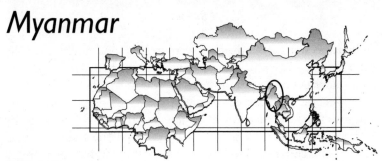

**Capital:** Yangon
**Population:** 49,800,000
**Languages:** Burmese, Karen, Shan
**Major Religions:** Buddhism, Christianity
**Major People Groups:** Bama (Burmese), Shan, Karen, Arakanese, Chinese
**Strategic Town or City:** Mandalay

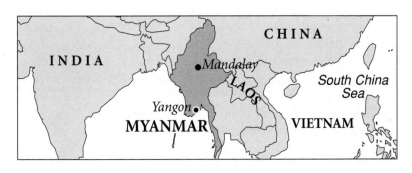

The growth of the church in Myanmar is an inspirational example of how one person can impact a nation. When Adoniram Judson sailed to South Asia in 1812, there were just a handful of Christians in Myanmar (known as Burma then). Today, there are 4.5 million believers! There is no memorial statue to Judson to be found anywhere in the land, but there are 4.5 million "living memorials" to the sacrifice and dedication of Judson and his family.

Myanmar is actually a collection of small kingdoms sur-rounded by mountains on three sides and the sea on the fourth. A rigid military government tightly controls Myanmar. Once part of the Mongol, Shan, and British empires, Myanmar is one of the wealthiest countries in Southeast Asia.

Buddhism is a major spiritual stronghold in the nation. Buddhist temples dot the landscape everywhere one looks. Though Adoniram Judson had a powerful influence on the country, it was primarily among the hill tribes; the gospel has yet to penetrate the more dominant Burmese people in a significant way.

The past 40 years in Myanmar have been filled with conflict between the Burmese-dominated government and the hill tribes that want independence. After a 1988 uprising, in which 3,000 protesters were killed, the government finally allowed free elections. Aung San Suu Kyi, the leader of the opposition party, won 85% of the vote but was placed under house arrest by the military. She won the Nobel Peace Prize in 1991 for her nonviolent efforts to bring democracy to Myanmar.

## Prayer Points

- Pray for freedom of political expression in Myanmar.
- Thank God for the witness of Jesus among the Karen and Kachin tribes. Ask God to send revival to the church so that fresh zeal for the lost and for missions will take root in the hearts of the believers.
- Intercede for a breakthrough among the Burmese people.
- Ask God to send a drug famine to the land and for the illegal trade in heroin to dry up. Pray for creative alternatives for the farmers.
- Lift up the need for a new wave of Adoniram Judsons to be sent out to Myanmar and all the lands of Southeast Asia.

# Chad

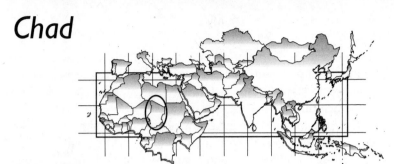

**Capital:** N'Djamena
**Population:** 6,200,000
**Languages:** French, Chadian Arabic, and over 100 other languages
**Major Religions:** Islam, Roman Catholicism, animism, Protestantism
**Major People Groups:** Sudanic, Chadian Arabs, Chadic, Saharan
**Strategic Town or City:** Moundou

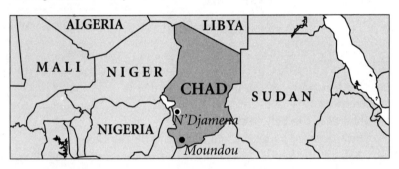

Since 1966 a major civil war has wrought havoc in Chad. Muslim groups in the north have fought government troops from the south. After numerous cease-fires and backing by the French government, Libyan troops, who were occupying the Aozou Strip in the north, withdrew from Chad in 1994, and a new constitution was approved in 1996. In 1990, the current president, Idriss Deby, came to power.

There are more unreached people groups in Chad than any other African country; 180 different people groups present tremendous opportunities for the spread of the gospel, but the diversity of languages, cultures, and tribal customs also present major challenges. Chad is in reality a confederation of many nations, and recognizing this is a helpful way to view the task of evangelizing the whole country.

The church in Chad grew rapidly in the 1960s and 1970s but experienced persecution from the government in the mid '70s. Many believers were martyred for their faith when they refused to participate in animistic rites. Famine, drought, and the civil war have made Chad a difficult place to live, but it is those same conditions that are a mandate for God's mercy.

Most of the easy places in the 10/40 Window have been reached! It is countries like Chad that present a serious challenge to us as believers to take up our cross and follow Jesus—to the hard places.

## Prayer Points

⌣· Let us believe God that many more servants of the Lord will take the challenge to reach the many unreached tribes of Chad. Pray for laborers! Pray for development workers, Bible translators, and church planters.

⌣· Ask God to prepare the soil of people's hearts for the seed of the gospel. May our Father in heaven use the harsh circumstances of drought, famine, and war to turn their hearts to Him.

⌣· Pray for mercy for Chad; let us ask God to alleviate the physical circumstances causing the suffering in Chad in such a way as to draw people's hearts to the Lord Jesus.

⌣· Pray for protection from growing Muslim influence.

⌣· Ask the Father for peace and reconciliation between tribes so the gospel can be preached.

⌣· Pray for the church: for appropriate and sensitive witness to Muslims; for indigenous pastors, church planters, and evangelists to be raised up; for hunger for God's Word; and for holiness.

⌣· Pray for nomadic people groups and those who live in remote desert villages and towns who are isolated from any witness of the gospel. Pray for people who are willing to lay down their lives in order to live and work for the glory of Jesus' Name in this challenging environment.

⌣· Pray for Chadian young people who have had Christian influence in their lives, that they will have a strong foundation in God's Word and that they will stand firm in Christ.

# Algeria

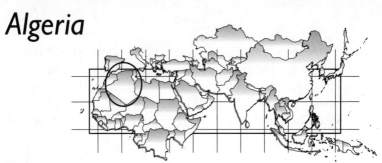

**Capital:** Algiers
**Population:** 33,700,000
**Languages:** Arabic, French, various Berber languages
**Major Religion:** Islam
**Major People Groups:** Algerian Arabs, Kabyle, Taznitit, Shawiya Berbers
**Strategic Town or City:** Wahran

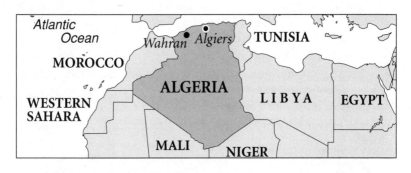

Algeria has experienced war and civil war for almost 50 years. Independence was gained from France in 1962 after a costly war to become free from colonial rule. Then, in 1992, the president of Algeria was assassinated. A protracted battle for control of the country ensued between Muslim fundamentalists and the army. Tens of thousands of people have lost their lives.

In spite of the turmoil, many people have come to Christ in Algeria. It is said that whole villages have been touched by the gospel. Some new believers testify to having seen the Lord in dreams and visions that were instrumental in leading them to Christ.

It seems that the Lord has withdrawn His restraining grace over this land and allowed the forces of darkness to turn on each other. The Bible says that God causes the wrath of men to praise Him. As you turn to prayer for this country, remember that what the enemy intended for harm against Joseph, God used for good. God does not cause evil, but He is greater than the greatest evil of men or Satan. Let us call out to God that He will turn the hearts of Algerian men and women to Himself and that He will use the violence of wicked men to create desperation in the hearts of people for divine intervention.

## Prayer Points

- Cry out to God with compassion for all those suffering because of the violence in Algeria. Pray for peace in Algeria.
- Ask God to give you and His church worldwide a broken heart for the suffering peoples of Algeria.
- Pray that the leaders of the various political factions would become willing to seek peace at all costs and begin to seek God for His help for their land.
- Pray that Jesus will be revealed to believers who are suffering and that they will be strengthened to persevere and be faithful to the Lord.
- Ask the Holy Spirit to raise up workers from other Berber peoples in North Africa to take the gospel to Algeria.
- Intercede for the many Algerians living in Europe—many of them in France.

# Libya

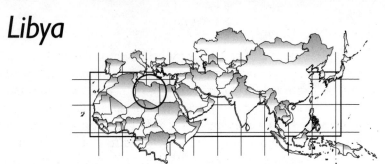

**Capital:** Tripoli
**Population:** 5,600,000
**Languages:** Libyan Arabic, some Berber languages
**Major Religion:** Islam
**Major People Groups:** Libyan Arabs and Berbers, Teda, Kel Tamasheq
**Strategic Town or City:** Banghazi

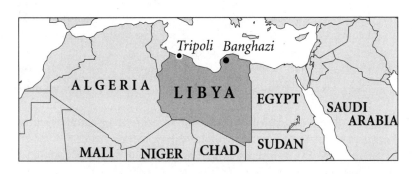

Alexander the Great conquered Libya in 322 B.C. The Romans ruled Libya after that, and during this period, Christianity spread to Libya. Simon the Cyrene, who carried the cross of Jesus, was from Libya (Cyrene was a small city on the Libyan coast). On the day of Pentecost, Cyrennians heard the gospel in their own language (Acts 2:10). For centuries this country has been dominated by foreign powers: the Phoenicians, Egyptians, Persians, Romans (for 500 years), Vandals, Arabs, Turks, and Italians. Foreigners have colonized Libya for so many years it is not surprising that a similar spirit influences its politics. The colonialism has reaped what it has sown in the spirit of the nation.

Libya is headed by the autocratic leader Muammar Kadhafi, who seeks to govern the country under principles of revolutionary socialism. He was brought into power in a coup in 1969 and, since that time, is believed to have sponsored various acts of terrorism outside of Libya's borders. Kadhafi used to be a fervent secularist, but now is encouraging his own brand of Islam in Libya and other countries. Opposition to Kadhafi's regime has come from militant Islamic and other opposition groups, many of whom have left the country.

The tense security and political situation has been known to hinder the witness of believers. Fear dominates the lives of Libyans; security forces are present in all parts of their society. In the midst of this, Libyans have shown openness to the gospel, but it is difficult to follow through. Since it is not an easy country to get into, radio and satellite television have a vital role in reaching the Libyan people.

## Prayer Points

- Pray that the Christian heritage of the Libyan people will be made known and revived. Only the power and mercy of God can break through the strongholds in Libya; pray that He would break the powers of darkness that hold the nation in bondage.
- Bless Muammar Kadhafi! We are told by the Lord Jesus to bless our enemies, and certainly this man has been outspoken against Christians at times. Heap blessings on him: blessings of God's love, revelations of Jesus, dreams and visions to visit him in the night. Pray for family members to hear the gospel on the radio, for Islamic leaders in Libya to meet genuine believers in their travels, and for God to put it on the heart of the right people to share the gospel with Kadhafi.
- Lift up the few Libyan believers inside and outside the country to be strengthened and empowered to share their faith. Ask the Lord to protect them from the snares of the evil one and for them to be grounded in the Word.

# Malaysia

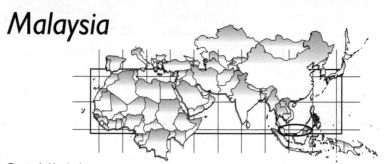

**Capital:** Kuala Lumpur
**Population:** 21,500,000
**Languages:** Malay, English, Chinese
**Major Religions:** Islam, Chinese religions, Christianity, Buddhism, Hinduism
**Major People Groups:** Malay, Chinese, tribal peoples, Indian
**Strategic Town:** Georgetown

Malaysia is a modern, prosperous nation that is one of the leading economies of the Pacific Rim. However, the Malay-dominated government has imposed restrictions against evangelism of Muslims. Those few Malays who are believers are subject to severe persecution, including death.

There are many churches in Malaysia, but they are for Chinese, Indian, and tribal peoples only. Those who dare share their faith with a Malay person may end up being reported to the police, and in some cases, accused of blasphemy against Mohammed, a very serious charge in any Muslim country.

Islam came to Malaysia in the 14th century from Northern Sumatra, and today the ethnic Malay people are 99.9% Muslim.

Malaysia is trying to carve out an image for itself of the "new Islam," a face of economic prosperity combined with adherence to conservative religious ideals.

Malaysia was ruled by both Dutch and British colonial powers for nearly 350 years. Malaysia gained independence from Britain in 1957, and since that time, the country has gained international prominence. Kuala Lumpur is a modern metropolis of high-rise apartment buildings, modern banks, and gleaming skyscrapers.

## Prayer Points

- Pray that the Chinese Christians will have wisdom and boldness in sharing their faith with Muslims. Believe God that they will not succumb to fear or unbelief, nor see the Muslims as their enemies.
- Ask God to bring renewal to Chinese churches scattered throughout the land, especially for vision to reach their neighbors and to send missionaries throughout the 10/40 Window.
- Ask God to reveal Himself to Malay government leaders, that their contact with Chinese Christians working in the government will stir hunger in their hearts for the gospel.
- There are several provinces populated primarily by tribal groups. Because they have no official religious affiliation, there is freedom to evangelize them. Ask God for laborers!
- Thank the Lord for the unique situation that exists in Malaysia as a Muslim land: Christians of one people group are free to associate with Muslims of another people group. God in His sovereignty has a plan that includes blessing all the peoples of Malaysia!

# Oman

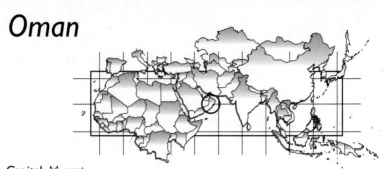

**Capital:** Muscat
**Population:** 2,100,000
**Language:** Arabic
**Major Religion:** Islam
**Major People Groups:** Omani Arab, Balochi, Pakistani
**Strategic Town or City:** Sur

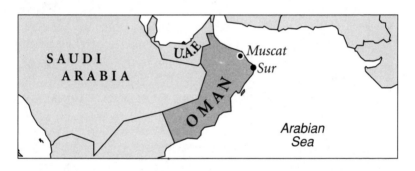

Oman is located on one of the world's busiest trade routes, along the coast of the Gulf of Oman and the Indian Ocean. The Persians ruled Oman until the country gained independence in 1744. At its height, their empire, known as Muscat and Oman, extended to both Africa and India.

Today the Omanis are ruled by an absolute monarchy, the Sultan Qaboos bin Said. Sultan Qaboos overthrew his father in 1970, and shortly thereafter he initiated the transformation that brought Oman into the 20th century. He developed the country's educational system, modern hospitals, a growing tourism industry, and greater economic opportunities. These developments provide many opportunities for expatriate Christians to reach out to

Omanis. In addition, about sixteen hundred Omanis study abroad each year.

For many centuries, Omanis have made their livelihood from the sea as sailors, fishermen, traders, and shipwrights. Now, Oman's wealth comes from its oil fields; however, they are expected to run dry in the next 10 to 20 years.

About 70% of the Omani workforce consists of foreigners. Most are guest workers from India, Pakistan, Bangladesh, Sri Lanka, Egypt, Jordan, and the Philippines. Many are non-Muslim, and some are believers working there as tentmakers. Expatriate believers have the freedom to worship in designated locations, although they are forbidden to evangelize Omanis. There are a handful of indigenous believers, but they are scattered and not worshipping together.

## Prayer Points

- Pray that God will overrule the powers of darkness that hold Omanis in bondage and reveal the light of the gospel to them.
- Ask the Father to raise up fellowships of believers to offer worship to His Son.
- Pray for an army of intercessors for Oman—men and women who will intercede until there are major breakthroughs.
- Ask the Lord for a great revival among the guest workers in Oman. Pray that signs and wonders will confirm the testimony they give to their faith in the Lord Jesus.
- Lift up the Christian radio broadcasts beamed into Oman in both Arabic and English. Some Omanis have come to Christ through these broadcasts.

# Kazakstan

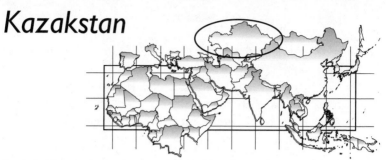

**Capital:** Akmola (recently moved from Alma-Ata)
**Population:** 18,200,000
**Languages:** Kazak, Russian, German
**Major Religions:** Islam, Russian Orthodox Christianity
**Major People Groups:** Kazak, Russian, German, Ukrainian, Uzbek, Uygur, Tatar
**Strategic Town or City:** Alma-Ata

Kazakstan is a huge land of deserts and forests, rich in minerals and natural resources. It is difficult to comprehend the vastness of Kazakstan, the largest of the former Soviet republics.

Thirty-six percent of the population is Russian, due to their occupation of Kazakstan since the middle part of the 19th century. Kazakstan has the largest Russian population of the former Soviet republics. When the nomadic Kazaks were forced into collective farms by the Soviets, nearly two million Kazaks died of starvation.

There is a remarkable level of freedom to share the gospel in Kazakstan; many Kazaks, and a growing number of Uygurs, have come to Christ since independence in 1991.

The former capital, Alma-Ata, is a cosmopolitan city of over 1.7 million inhabitants. Surrounded by the Tian Shan Mountains, Alma-Ata is now struggling with the big city problems of pollution, crime, and family disintegration. However, God is working mightily all over Kazakstan, and people are very open to the gospel. One Christian worker in a metropolitan area started a church with only four believers. Less than three years later, there are forty members and the small church is thriving. Shortly after coming to Christ herself, one young woman stood before her fellow believers and tearfully entreated them to continue to reach out to Kazak young people.

Turkey, Saudi Arabia, and Iran are vying for religious and economic influence in Kazakstan. Kazakstan needs help in developing its natural resources, but even more it needs protection from those seeking to exploit the country for their own purposes. Please join your voice with millions of other believers as we stand with our brothers and sisters around the world in blessing this beautiful land.

## Prayer Points

- Pray for continued favor and anointing to reach the minority groups in Kazakstan with the gospel.
- Intercede that outsiders with their own agendas would not exploit the indigenous church. Lift up the growing church and that Kazak leaders will be raised up to lead the church.
- Pray for a mission vision among Kazak believers and that God will raise up Kazak evangelists, pastors, and church planters.
- Pray for protection for the Kazak government and peoples from outside exploitation and domination.
- Please stand against the enemy as he seeks to oppress the Kazak people with fear, spiritism, and growing materialism.
- Ask God in prayer to show you the tactics of the enemy against God's people in Kazakstan. Pray against these tactics in faith, knowing the Lord has a great plan to use the Kazak people to reach the nations with the gospel!

# Tunisia

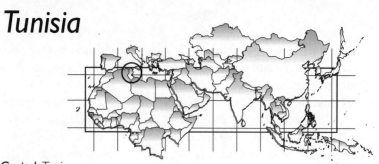

**Capital:** Tunis
**Population:** 10,100,000
**Languages:** Arabic, French
**Major Religion:** Islam
**Major People Groups:** Arab, Arabic Berber
**Strategic Town or City:** Sfax

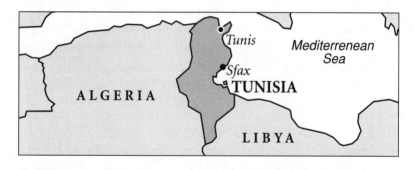

Located in North Africa between Libya and Algeria, the tiny country of Tunisia was part of the ancient empire of Carthage, which once dominated trade in the Mediterranean. In Roman times, it was the site of a flourishing church that became one of the centers of Latin Christianity, producing teachers—such as Tertullian, Cyprian, and Augustine—who shaped Western theology for centuries to come. However, after the arrival of Islam in the seventh century, the church soon disappeared. Today, despite over 100 years of Christian missionary effort, the church in Tunisia still has not been reestablished. Recent efforts have been frustrated by materialism and spiritual apathy in society, division in the church, and spiritual attack and police pressure on believers.

Tunisia is a very secular and almost Westernized country. The government has actively repressed Islamic fundamentalism and any expression of Christianity. At present, Tunisia is a tourist haven for Europeans, with charters landing daily from Spain, Germany, and England. The people are friendly and open to out-siders, but the repressive policies of the government have made it very difficult for local believers to gather for worship or to share their faith.

## *Prayer Points*

- Lift up the local believers and expatriate Christians serving in Tunisia, that they will be protected from fear and grow in the holy boldness they already demonstrate.
- Pray for the government leaders to give freedom of religion to Christians.
- Intercede that the forces of Islamic fundamentalism would be overthrown spiritually, and for student leaders to be con-verted to faith in Christ.
- Pray for a revival of signs and wonders to break out in villages and on the university campuses, testifying to the reality of the resurrected Christ.
- Ask the Holy Spirit to raise up missionaries from other nations to go to Tunisia.
- Ask God to protect the unity of missionary organizations working together throughout North Africa, and to give them hope and faith to reach North Africa.

# Cambodia

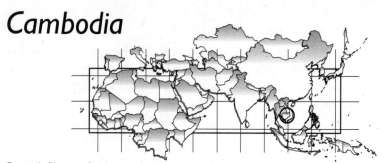

**Capital:** Phnom Penh
**Population:** 8,500,000
**Languages:** Khmer and French
**Major Religion:** Buddhism
**Major People Groups:** Khmer, Chinese, Vietnamese
**Strategic Town or City:** Betdambang

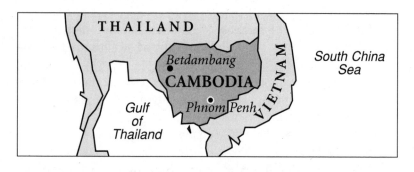

Sadly, the *killing fields of Cambodia, Pol Pot,* and the *Khmer Rouge* are household words around the world. The Khmer Rouge evacuated all the cities and towns of Cambodia and killed over two million people in its reign of terror, including most of the Christians, government leaders, and intellectuals.

Out of this nightmare, the church was born in Cambodia. Tens of thousands of Cambodians, especially young people, turned to Christ. Churches were planted by the scores in refugee camps along the Thai-Kampuchean border.

But this does not mean Cambodia is a Christian country. Buddhism still holds an iron grip on the hearts of most Cambodians. Both Hinduism and Buddhism came to Cambodia through merchants traveling between China and India. Legend has it that the ancient Khmer king Jayavarman II was given divine status by the Hindu god Shiva, the ultimate source of chaos and destruction. Cambodia's bloody history seems to reflect this spiritual allegiance.

## Prayer Points

- Lift up the church of Jesus among the Khmer people scattered as refugees around the world, especially in the United States. Ask God to rekindle the fires of evangelistic passion and desperation for God that led to the church being planted in the first place.
- Pray for workers to go through the open doors to work in Cambodia today. The land is scarred with the aftermath of war, and the hearts of the people are wounded. Infrastructure is being established throughout the land; there is a great need for community development and primary healthcare workers who have a burden to share the gospel and plant churches.
- Cambodia is littered with land mines. Pray for the safe removal of these mines, and especially for the safety of the children.
- Pray for converted refugees who are now pastors, evangelists, and church planters to return to Cambodia from the United States and other countries where they are now living. Cambodia needs missionaries and workers!
- Ask God to pull down the demonic powers of violence and destruction that have inflicted this land since they gained a foothold many centuries ago.
- Ask the Lord to release indigenous worship through the church, so that Jesus is lifted up in ways that are of Cambodian culture, and not an import from other places.

# Turkey

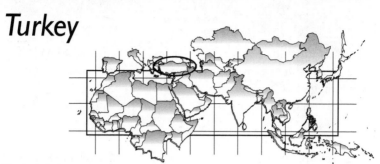

**Capital:** Ankara
**Population:** 69,000,000
**Languages:** Turkish, Kurdish, Arabic
**Major Religion:** Islam
**Major People Groups:** Turk, Kurd, Azeri, Tatar, Gypsy
**Strategic Town or City:** Istanbul

Abrahim was short, broad chested, and fearless. Yet, inner turmoil was driving him to the point of desperation. He missed his wife and sons back in the little village he came from in the mountains of central Turkey. Abrahim was a shepherd by trade but was working in Germany to support his extended family back home. He longed for the quiet hills and close family life he'd left behind.

By "chance" Abrahim dropped into a Christian coffee bar late one night in Berlin, on his way to take his life. He was deeply touched by the sincerity of the Christians and readily accepted a Scripture portion offered to him by one of the Christians. Months later, in a "chance" encounter with a believer who was present the night he visited the coffee bar, Abrahim gave his heart to the Lord.

Millions of Turks just like Abrahim are scattered throughout Western Europe, alienated from their host cultures but unable to fit back into the harsh village life they come from. Like their fellow countrymen back home, they are increasingly being confronted with the gospel of Jesus Christ. This is a key time in the history of Turkey; once again the gospel is being proclaimed in the area Paul preached in on his second missionary journey.

Hundreds of Christians, motivated by the love of Christ, are serving in Turkey today. Over 1,000 Turks have responded personally to the claims of Jesus Christ. From a nation that had less than 50 known believers and fewer than 25 Christian workers twenty years ago, Turkey is the focus of a resurgence of Christian activity.

Kemal Ataturk founded the modern nation of Turkey in 1923 on principles of secularism and religious moderation. And though it is still an overwhelmingly Muslim nation, Turkish believers are beginning to stand up for their faith. Churches are being registered, and individual believers are starting to resist religious discrimination.

A remarkable contribution to the new spiritual awakening that is beginning to surface in Turkey is the "Reconciliation Walk" of Christians, retracing the routes of the crusaders. Hundreds of Christians have walked and prayed on the same roads traveled by the crusaders over 900 years ago, asking forgiveness from mayors, Muslim clerics, and every person they meet for the many horrendous acts of violence and hatred done in the name of Christ during the crusades. The response has been overwhelming.

Turkey is looked up to by many Muslim nations in Central Asia and the Middle East. Many trace their languages and cultures back to the Ottoman Empire. Those nations seeking an alternative to the fundamentalism of Iran or the extremism of Saudi Arabia consider Turkey an example of secular Islamic government and modern progress. Turkish Islamic missionaries are active throughout Central Asia.

If Turkey was captured for Christ, it is hard to imagine what effect it would have on the rest of the Muslim world. Let us join our prayers with millions of other believers in blessing the peoples of Turkey. May God grant such a move of His Spirit in this land that millions will come to know Him as their Lord and Savior.

## *Prayer Points*

- Pray for the seed of the gospel that has been planted in the hearts of millions of Turks, through the Reconciliation Walks, to be protected and bear fruit.
- Ask our Father for the Turkish believers to be strong and pure in their faith. Pray for a spirit of revival and holiness in His church.
- Pray for unity among Christian workers and believers in Turkey. Pray against a spirit of division, mistrust, and gossip.
- Intercede fervently for many thousands more Turks to come into the Kingdom of God.
- Join in prayer with those who are spearheading a project to see a church planted in all 80 provinces of Turkey. Stand against the enemy's attempts to thwart God's purposes, and especially pray for protection for those leading this project.
- Ask God to overturn the plans the enemy has to infiltrate Turkey with a spirit of Islamic fundamentalism and violence.

# North Korea

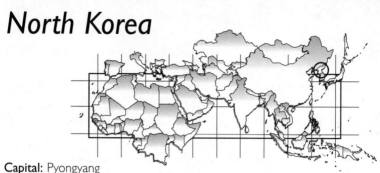

**Capital:** Pyongyang
**Population:** 24,900,000
**Language:** Korean
**Major Religion:** None, but there is a powerful and growing underground church
**Major People Group:** Korean
**Strategic Town or City:** Ch'ongjin

After decades of isolation from the rest of the world, North Korea has been forced to emerge from its political and psychological cocoon. Famine, economic crisis, and the death of their leader thrust North Korea into dialogue with the United States, Japan, and South Korea. However, the will of the political leaders is still not broken. North Korea is one of the world's last Communist strongholds.

Legend has it that Tangun founded Korea in 2333 B.C. He was revered as both king and god. Today, many North Koreans still treat their leaders with the reverence due a god. Tangun's descendents reigned over the peaceful kingdom for the next millennium, although since then the Korean peninsula has been divided a number of times. After the Korean War of the 1950s, it was divided again.

Many Christians in North Korea have either been martyred or fled to the south. While the church in South Korea has exploded in size, religious expression in the North has been brutally repressed.

In the last few years, the famine situation in North Korea has forced open the doors to visitors. They have reported unimaginable devastation and loss of human life. Some estimate that up to 30% of the population has died. What better time is there for us to lift North Korea before the throne of God in concerted prayer?

## Prayer Points

⌣· Ask God to give the people of North Korea freedom from political oppression so that hunger for spiritual things would be allowed free expression.

⌣· There is an underground church in North Korea—lift our brothers and sisters before the Lord. They have suffered greatly and are in constant danger of exposure and death.

⌣· North Korea suffers from ethnic isolation, cut off from the rest of the world. This is fostered by pride and fear. Ask the Father to break down the walls of mistrust and fear and reveal to North Koreans how loved they are by others in the world. Demonic powers are attacking this nation by trying to keep it isolated from the rest of the world. Let us come against that spirit by blessing the beloved and special people of North Korea.

# Somalia

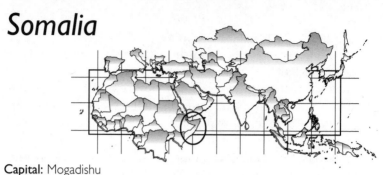

**Capital:** Mogadishu
**Population:** 12,560,000
**Languages:** Somali, Arabic
**Major Religion:** Islam
**Major People Group:** Somali
**Strategic Town or City:** Kismaayo

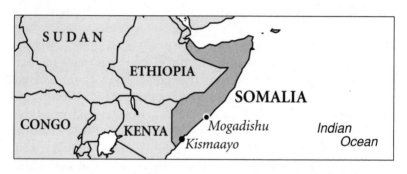

Clan loyalty and clan fighting are the driving forces of Somali life. In 1969, General Mohammed Siad Barre seized power and imposed a one-man rule. In 1974, he evicted missionary organizations from the country, but in 1991 he himself ran for his life as rival clans chased him out of Somalia. The country then disintegrated into interclan fighting, resulting in man-made famine and devastation. In 1992 the United Nations and US failed in their joint attempt to reestablish stability within the country.

Somalia remains war-torn and divided. Many missionaries returned under Christian aid agencies to care for refugees and give witness to the gospel in spite of the great danger involved. However, in recent years most have been forced to evacuate due to the great instability of the country.

The Somalis believe their first ancestor was a member of the Qaraysh (Koreish) tribe, to which the prophet Mohammed belonged. Somalia is almost completely a Muslim country. Christian believers are very few and scattered, and in recent years, some have been martyred for their faith. At present, there is no viable indigenous church.

Somalia is an oral culture, with a high value on poetry, proverbs, and traditional stories. As a point of clan identity, children memorize their genealogies for several generations. Memorization was vital, as their language was not in written form until 1974. It is a point of honor for Somali storytellers to memorize their story accurately and recite it clearly. Thus, storytelling is a highly effective way to communicate the gospel.

## Prayer Points

- Pray for peace in Somalia and that clan leaders would repent for the devastation they have caused to the land.
- Lift up the hundreds of thousands of Somali refugees all over the world. Pray for openness to the gospel as they are exposed to Christianity in their new environments.
- Ask God to raise up an indigenous church in Somalia and to protect it from the factionalism that divides the people from each other.
- Pray for the Christian aid agencies working with Somalis both in Somalia and surrounding countries, and for the workers who are exposed to frequent danger.
- Intercede fervently for the salvation of Somali poets and storytellers who could communicate the gospel to the clans and people of Somalia.

# Pakistan

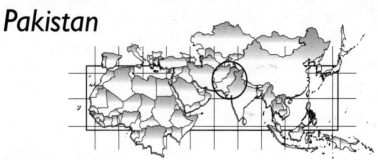

**Capital:** Islamabad
**Population:** 149,100,000
**Languages:** Urdu, Pushtun, Kashmiri, many others
**Major Religions:** Islam, Protestant Christianity
**Major People Groups:** Punjabi, Sindhi, Baluch, Pushtu, Kashmiri
**Strategic Town or City:** Karachi

The modern nation of Pakistan was formed in 1947 in a bloody struggle for partition from India. For a while, Pakistan and Bangladesh were one nation (West and East Pakistan), but the distance both in miles and in culture made this arrangement untenable. Bangladesh gained independence in 1971 after a brutal civil war. Millions of lives were lost in the struggle for Pakistan and Bangladesh to become independent countries.

There is a growing church in Pakistan, but opposition from Muslim fundamentalists makes it very difficult. Officially, it is illegal for Muslims to convert to Christianity. In recent years, Christians have lost their lives by being falsely accused of criticizing the Koran or speaking against Muhammad.

There are churches being started amongst political refugees from other countries in Pakistan, but this is a very sensitive issue for the government.

Pakistan is the third largest Islamic nation in the world and has the potential for vast influence if a revival broke out.

## Prayer Points

- The tension in the last two years between India and Pakistan has grown because of the development of nuclear weapons. Pray for peace.
- Intercede for the church in Pakistan; pray for the fear of God and for freedom from the fear of man. May God revive His church in Pakistan, and may many be raised up who will fearlessly proclaim the Name of Christ. Pray for doors to be opened for creative ways to reach Muslims with the gospel.
- Pray for whole tribal peoples in the north to come to Christ. Doors are open and workers are needed.
- Millions of refugees from Afghanistan have come to Pakistan. Pray that God will use the oppression of the Taliban fundamentalists in Afghanistan to open up the hearts of these refugees to the gospel. Pray for the Afghan church in Pakistan to be strong.
- Ask the Lord of the Harvest to raise up workers: for creative doors to be opened, and for wisdom and boldness in proclaiming the gospel.
- Pray for the city of Karachi, where violence and bloodshed are common. It is a wicked port city, with many political and criminal factions vying for control of the wealth that is there.

# Nigeria

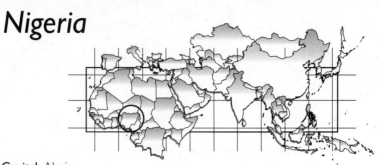

**Capital:** Abuja
**Population:** 160,800,000
**Languages:** English, Hausa, Yoruba, Ibo
**Major Religions:** Islam, Christianity, animism
**Major People Groups:** Hausa, Yoruba, Ibo
**Strategic Town or City:** Lagos

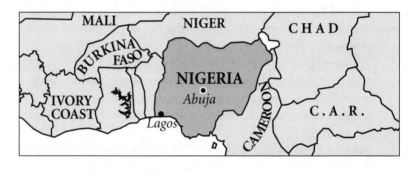

Nigeria is a nation of some 100 million people and is a feder-ation of 30 states. It was a British colony until 1960. Since then, a succession of military, Muslim-dominated governments have been in power, but a transition to democratic, civilian rule is under way.

There are wide cultural differences among Nigerians. The north is primarily Muslim while the south is largely Christian. This creates an open door the Lord can use to spread the gospel into the Muslim nations of North Africa. Nigeria has one of the largest Christian populations of all the countries in the 10/40 Window. In addition, the nation has the economic and spiritual resources necessary for reaching other nations. There are several outstanding indigenous missionary organizations that send workers from there to the nations.

Slavery, kidnapping, murder, and witchcraft are all part of Nigeria's history. Since its independence from Britain in 1960, this nation suffered often under an iron hand of military rule, and it currently is staggering under foreign debt and high inflation. Islam is widespread. Fear of persecution keeps many who have rejected Islam from publicly converting to Christianity. When people do become Christians, they often blend their tribal religious beliefs with those of the church. In addition, struggles among the 250 ethnic groups and various forms of occult worship are commonplace.

## Prayer Points

- Lift up the need for honest people in the nation, people who will not accept bribes and cannot be bought at any price. Ask the Lord to bring conviction of sin where dishonesty and corruption has seeped into the church.
- Nigeria is a nation of leaders; you can find Nigerians all over the world doing business and excelling at education and industry. Pray that Nigerians will hear the call to reach the lost in the unreached nations of the world and provide a new wave of spiritual leaders to go to the neediest places on the planet.
- There is tremendous tension between the Muslim-dominated military and Christians in politics and commerce. Pray for the deep divisions in Nigeria to be healed and for Christian leaders to have proactive answers for Nigeria's future.
- Pray for peace between the Christian south and the Muslim north. Many pastors have been killed, churches burned, and believers persecuted.

# Maldives

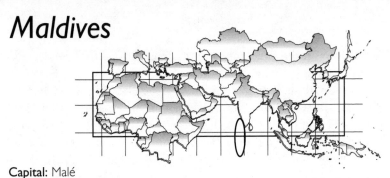

**Capital:** Malé
**Population:** 300,000
**Language:** Divehi
**Major Religion:** Islam
**Major People Group:** Maldivian
**Strategic Town or City:** Malé

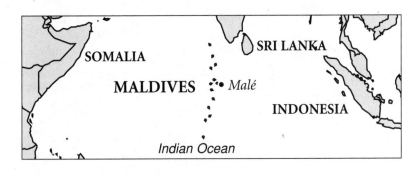

Upcoming elections in this tiny island nation have led to the expulsion of most Christian workers serving the Maldivian people with the love of Christ. Local believers have been arrested and the secret police have stepped up their scrutiny of all those suspected of being "influenced" by outsiders. One ten-year-old boy unwittingly turned in his mother, a believer, for Christian activity, and she is now being interrogated by the police. Other believers have also been arrested. The Maldives claims to be 100% Muslim, so as non-Muslims under the Maldivian constitution, the believers there have no rights whatsoever. The prisoners are being held captive in the notorious political prison-island of Dhoonidhoo. Their position is extremely vulnerable because the Maldivian authorities hide what is happening and claim that no such persons exist.

In spite of death threats, a believer living outside the country continues to record radio programs being broadcast into the Maldives. These programs have been received very enthusiastically by the local people but, because of their Christian content, are now being jammed by the government.

The Maldives are a long string of mostly uninhabited islands lying off the southwest coast of India. There are over 1,000 islands that make up this tropical paradise, but only about 200 of them are inhabited. The Portuguese, Dutch, and British have colonized the Maldives over the last 400 years. They received their independence in 1965. The Maldivian people are a mixture of Indian, Sinhalese, and Arab ethnicity but now have their own sense of identity as a people.

The Maldives are a fiercely controlled Islamic state, and until twenty years ago, were listed as one of a handful of nations with no known believers. Due to a barrage of prayer from around the world, and the attention given to the unreached people groups of the 10/40 Window, that has now changed!

The Maldives are open to tourism: 747s take off weekly from London and Johannesburg, filled with honeymooners and tourists seeking to enjoy this island paradise's fantastic beaches and resorts. Tourists have contact with hotel workers and tour guides but are not allowed to visit the outlying inhabited islands without a government permit and a tour guide.

Spiritism, fear, suspicion, and government control characterize the spiritual climate in the Maldives. It is reported that the divorce rate in the Maldives is one of the highest in the world. (Divorce is easy to obtain for a Muslim man; all he has to do is repeat the phrase "I divorce you" three times and he is free from obligation. This leaves the woman with a terrible stigma and in total dependence on others.)

God is working in the Maldives, and the recent spiritual attacks are a sign that the forces of darkness are being defeated. It is time to step up our prayer and spiritual warfare on behalf of these wonderful people!

## Prayer Points

- Intercede for the radio broadcasts being beamed into the Maldives to be heard in all the islands and for government efforts to jam them to fail. Pray for the people producing these broadcasts to be protected and for renewed courage and boldness.

- Please pray fervently for the believers meeting secretly to be guarded by angels and to be kept from harm. Pray for those being persecuted for their faith, and those held in prison, that their "faith fail not."

- Lift up those Maldivians working in the tourist industry to hear the gospel, accept Christ, and evangelize others of their own people. (They have greater freedom to travel.)

- Pray for Christian workers expelled from the Maldives because of their faith, and for renewed vision for reaching the Maldivian people.

- Join your voices today with other believers around the world against poverty, spiritism, divorce, and ungodly influences from Western tourists. May God bless the preaching of the gospel to the Maldivian people; He alone can solve the spiritual and social challenges facing this nation.

- Pray fervently in faith for government leaders to be saved! And pray that they would see Christianity as a blessing and not a curse for their land.

# Jordan

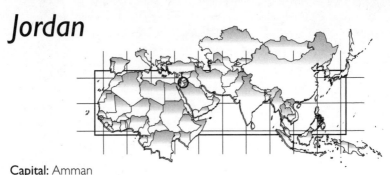

**Capital:** Amman
**Population:** 5,700,000
**Language:** Arabic
**Major Religion:** Islam
**Major People Groups:** Palestinian, Jordanian Arab
**Strategic Town or City:** Az-zarqa

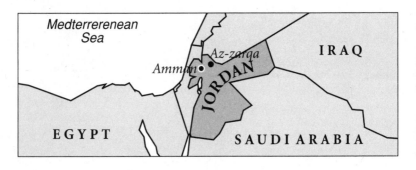

Jordan is nestled in the Middle East alongside some big and influential neighbors, including Israel, Syria, Iraq, Egypt, and Saudi Arabia. Jordan was part of the Turkish Empire until 1918, then gained independence from Great Britain in 1946 when it became a constitutional monarchy with King Hussein as its leader.

The recent Gulf War and the sanctions that followed have taken a disastrous economic toll on the nation and have unsettled political life. After the war, many Jordanians began to question the relevance and truth of Islam. Unprecedented openness resulted in many conversions to Christ! The *Jesus* film and other Christian television and radio programs have had a significant impact. God is at work in Jordan!

Islam is still the official religion in Jordan, and although Muslims are not allowed to change their religion, the constitution forbids discrimination and promotes the free exercise of religious beliefs and worship.

The royal family of Jordan descends from the Hashemites, the same family as the prophet Mohammed. The British placed them in leadership because of their political and religious power. There is pressure on the royal family from the Muslim brotherhood and the large number of Palestinians living in Jordan.

## Prayer Points

- Pray that extremist Muslim groups would not gain greater influence or power in Jordan.
- Lift up the church in Jordan, especially for greater unity and for a spirit of brokenness.
- Ask God to give the believers in Jordan boldness to share their faith in Christ, and for their witness to be followed by signs and wonders. May the church of Jesus grow and multiply in Jordan! Let us believe for many more churches to be planted and filled with men and women who will find Christ for the first time!
- Intercede for the royal family, especially for King Hussein, who is suffering from cancer. May God heal his body and open his heart to the love of the Lord Jesus. The king took the throne when he was only 15 years old, having survived assassins' bullets and much political turmoil.
- Pray for the Palestinian people in Jordan. They long for a homeland, and feel the "Christian" West has sided unfairly with Israel, ignoring their desires and rights to a homeland as well. There are many believers among the Palestinians.

# Senegal

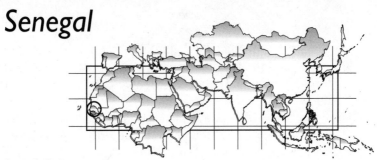

**Capital:** Dakar
**Population:** 9,700,000
**Language:** French
**Major Religion:** Islam
**Major People Groups:** Wolof, Fulani, Jola
**Strategic Town or City:** Thies

Senegal, located in West Africa, was ruled by Ghana in the 9th century and by Mali in the 13th century. Between these two occupations, Moroccan invaders brought Islam to Senegal. Senegal gained independence from France in 1960 and today has a constitutional form of government. Unfortunately, Senegal is currently on the verge of economic collapse, with over two thirds of the population unemployed. Many in the upper class are greedy, leaving the rest of the people struggling against poverty.

Since its independence from France, the Muslim religion has spread rapidly throughout Senegal, with about 92% of its people becoming Muslims. The entire region contains almost 100 million Muslims and their number continues to grow.

Local Muslim holy men known as Marabouts dominate Islam in Senegal. They are reputed to be channels of the blessing of God and mediators of salvation through spiritual descent from Mohammed. They are also the main source of magic charms, curses, and sorcery, giving them great power and prestige in the community. To a large degree, Islam in Senegal is enmeshed with tribal religions.

The few missionaries stationed in Senegal say they have witnessed a spiritual softening toward the gospel of Jesus in recent years. Although people's hearts may be softening, their eyes are still blind to the truth.

There are over 50 ethnic groups in Senegal, the majority of whom are Muslim. Allegiance to religious societies and the Marabouts is so strong that it makes it very difficult to reach these unreached people groups with the gospel.

## Prayer Points

⌣· The largest people groups in Senegal are the Wolof, Fulani, and Jola. There are few believers among them, and all three of these people groups desperately need the gospel. Pray for laborers! Pray for people who will die to familiar food, comfort, security, and home, for men and women who will follow Jesus into the desert places!

⌣· Drought and famine have stricken the nations of West Africa with a vengeance. Ask God to be merciful to Senegal and give her one more chance to hear about His Son, Jesus. God hears desperate, fervent prayers. Let us pray as if the lives of these people depend on us.

⌣· There are few believers in Senegal, and they need discipleship. Ask the Lord to raise up pastors and teachers for His church in Senegal.

# Eritrea

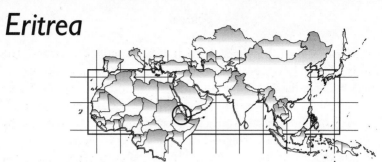

**Capital:** Asmara
**Population:** 4,600,000
**Languages:** Tigrinya, Tigre, English
**Major Religions:** Islam, Orthodox Christianity
**Major People Groups:** Tigrinya, Afar, Tigre, Mensa, and many others
**Strategic Town of City:** Mitsiwa

Eritrea's history is intertwined with that of Ethiopia, from which it is newly independent. Eritrea was part of the Ethiopian kingdom of Aksum, an Italian colony for many years until it was captured by the British. After a period of United Nations supervision, Eritrea was awarded to Ethiopia in 1952, but the arrangement did not last. After 31 years of fierce fighting, Eritrea formally declared itself an independent nation in 1993.

Eritreans have proven themselves to be survivors. They are a proud, independent people with a strong commitment to working together for the good of the country. The cooperation between the diverse ethnic peoples and religious groups in Eritrea is unusual. The Tigre, who are almost entirely Muslim, have a Bible in their language but few Christians among them, while the Tigrinya people are predominantly Christian.

## *Prayer Points*

⌣· Ask the Lord to continue to bless Eritrea with national unity so the gospel can be spread.

⌣· Many people groups within Eritrea remain unreached. Ask the Lord for workers to be raised up, especially among the Afar, Nara, Beja, and Saho.

⌣· Eritrea is still rebuilding after many years of war; intercede for healing for the land, for the rebuilding of the infrastructure, development of agriculture, reintegration of refugees, and rebuilding of churches.

⌣· Pray for the leaders of the church in Eritrea to be free from compromise and corruption and for the believers to be mobilized to carry the gospel to other people groups and lands.

⌣· Ask the Lord to bring healing to the hearts of those who lost loved ones during the years of fighting.

# Tibet

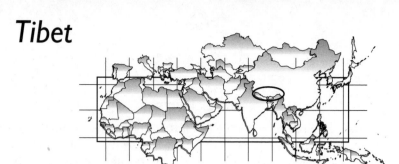

**Capital:** Lhasa
**Population:** 2,400,000
**Languages:** Tibetan (Lhasa, Amdo, and Khamba), Mandarin Chinese
**Major Religion:** Lamaist Buddhism
**Major People Groups:** Monda, Lhoba, Qiang
**Strategic Towns or Cities:** Lhasa

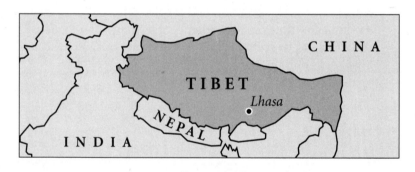

Tibet is a Buddhist stronghold, practicing one of the darkest forms of religion on the earth today. Demonic powers grip the hearts of the people of Tibet. The Buddhist temples stay busy with a steady stream of pilgrims making offerings, leaving prayer flags, and chanting to their gods.

The Dalai Lama is the highest spiritual and political leader in Tibet, and he is revered as a god—considered to be the reincarnation of Buddha himself. He fled Tibet after the Chinese occupation and now lives in India. He leads an international crusade against Chinese occupation of Tibet. His pleas for help have drawn international attention, and he has become a cause cèlébre in Hollywood.

Tibet is virtually unreached with the gospel. Few Tibetans have made a commitment to Christ, although there is a small underground church. The Tibetans are particularly difficult to reach because of their nomadic lifestyles and hard-to-learn languages. Because of the persecution by the Chinese and the attempt to crush their religion, Tibetans are resistant to outside influence and afraid of losing their identity as Tibetans. To be Tibetan is to be Buddhist, in their understanding.

However, God intervenes in Tibetan lives in miraculous ways! Several years ago, a missionary was on a short-term outreach to Tibet, trekking through the mountains, visiting villages and sharing the gospel. In one village, the group encountered an eight-year-old girl who was crippled and couldn't walk. The Christians prayed for the child and moved on to the next village. The missionary always wondered what had happened to her.

Many years later, he found out. By divine appointment, the man met the girl, now in her twenties, in another part of the country. She recognized him as one of those who had prayed for her and told him that, as the result of their prayers, she had been completely healed! This kept her from committing to Buddhism, and eventually she met other missionaries who introduced her to the God who had healed her. She stood before the man now as his sister in Christ, and together they praised the Lord for His goodness!

Pray against the strongholds of Tibet; ask the Father of all creation to unleash His great power and mercy over this land. May Jesus Christ be worshipped in every valley and on every mountaintop of Tibet!

## Prayer Points

- Pray for peace and freedom in Tibet. Let us believe God that the Tibetan people will be freed from political oppression, so the gospel will be spread throughout the land.
- Thank the Lord for the many Christians around the world that are reaching out to the Tibetan people. Many Tibetans live in India; large concentrations of them can also be found in Nepal and Bhutan. Ask the Lord of the Harvest to raise up many more laborers who will go, especially Tibetan believers!

- Intercede that Christian radio broadcasts, Scripture portions, tracts, evangelistic trekking teams, government personnel, and nongovernment workers will all be used mightily to break down the walls of ignorance and demonic oppression that blind the eyes of the Tibetan people to the truth of God's love.
- Pray especially for Scripture to be translated into a common, easy-to-understand language, as the common people cannot read the literary language used for a holy book such as the Bible.
- Pray for government officials to welcome small businesses, university students, and teachers to their land, and that believers will hear about the opportunities and go!
- Pray especially for opportunities for missionaries to work among the nomadic tribes and plant churches there.
- Intercede for Tibetan believers who face persecution from their families as extreme as poisoning and stoning. Pray for protection and strength for them.

# Syria

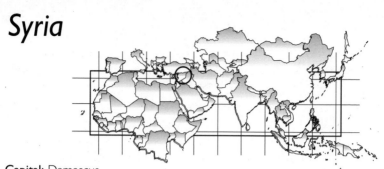

**Capital:** Damascus
**Population:** 18,000,000
**Languages:** Arabic, Kurdish
**Major Religions:** Islam, Orthodox Christianity
**Major People Groups:** Arab, Kurd, Turk, Assyrian
**Strategic Town of City:** Halab

The following words from the Bible are found inscribed over the entrance of the Umayyad Mosque in Damascus: "His kingdom is an eternal kingdom; His domain endures from generation to generation" (from Dan. 4:3). Previously, the mosque was the Cathedral of John the Baptist. Now it is one of the oldest and most revered shrines in Islam.

The political situation in Syria is complex and fraught with danger. Everything is not what it seems; though Islam was dropped as the state religion in 1973, and officially there is freedom of religion, more than 90% of the people remain Muslims. The government closely monitors all activities by believers, making it difficult to evangelize in this environment.

Like most Middle Eastern countries, Syria has experienced war and political upheaval in recent decades. Influence from fundamentalist Islam has turned Syria into a dangerous place to live. Many Christians have fled for their safety and a better life. There are very few Christian workers.

The collapse of the Soviet Union and the Gulf War have both had a profound impact on Syria's traditional anti-Western posture. The collapse of the USSR deprived Syria of significant foreign aid and political support, and the Gulf War highlighted the rewards of participatory politics and isolated the more radical elements in the Muslim world. We must pray that Syria will continue to open up to the outside world and welcome Christian personnel and guest workers from other lands.

Syria is a dynamic country, rapidly entering the modern world of technology and economic development, but at the same time maintaining ties to its ancient traditions. Damascus has been a hub of trade and commerce for thousands of years in the Middle East and claims to be the world's oldest capital. Saul of Tarsus was converted in Damascus, on his way to persecute Christians, when he had a blinding vision of the Lord (Acts 9). For the next several centuries, Syria was a center for Christian activity and influence. Syria became a Muslim country in the seventh century.

Syria still harbors some of the most radical Palestinian elements. With the declining health of President Hafaz al-Assad, the country could be quickly taken over by radical extremists if he were to die suddenly.

God wants to build His church in Syria and see many more churches planted and multiplied throughout the land. Satan wants to isolate Syria and create havoc through fear and hatred of outsiders. Today is the day to see the plans of the enemy exposed for what they are and to see Syria experience a new beginning in God.

## Prayer Points

- Pray against Syria's isolation from the rest of the world. Ask God to lift the fear and bitterness from the hearts of the people toward Israel, and America in particular, and for God's peace to come to the land.

⌣· Pray against the radical elements in Syria gaining control of the country.

⌣· Pray blessings upon the president of Syria. In the latter years of his life, may God grant him mercy and grace and a revelation of His great love.

⌣· Pray for revival among Syrian believers, that they would experience the reality of God's love. Ask God to pour out on them fresh zeal for the gospel and great compassion for their neighbors and friends. Pray for a spirit of boldness and sacrifice.

⌣· Pray for laborers to go to Syria, especially for church planters to gain access to the country. May God build His church!

# Mongolia

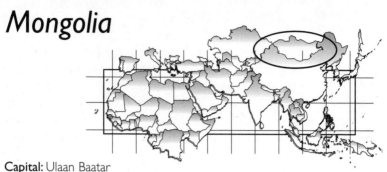

**Capital:** Ulaan Baatar
**Population:** 2,800,000
**Language:** Kalka Mongolian
**Major Religions:** Atheism, Lamaistic Buddhism, Islam
**Major People Groups:** Mongolian, Russian, Kazak
**Strategic Town or City:** Darhan

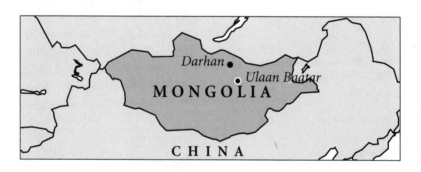

From a few converts led to Christ by James Gilmore of the London Missionary Society in the early 1870s, to over 10,000 Mongolian believers today, Mongolia is experiencing a major movement to Christ. Three months after Mongolia gained independence in 1990, a small team arrived in Ulaan Baatar whose members included four different tribes of Native Americans. The Native American believers created a cultural bridge to the gospel, which resulted in two Mongols being baptized. By August of 1991, the Mongol church had grown to more than 200 believers. That number multiplied to over 1,000 by the end of 1992. By April of 1998, it was conservatively estimated that there were 10,000 Mongol believers—and the church is still growing!

The largest church in Mongolia is in the city of Erdenet, with over 800 believers, 12 daughter churches, and 50 cell groups! This church is completely Mongolian led and has been an example of what God can do when missionaries cooperate with the Holy Spirit and apply cross-cultural principles of church growth. From the beginning, the missionary team in Erdenet was committed to plant an indigenous church. Mongolian leaders were recognized and released, and believers were encouraged to contextualize the gospel.

Modern-day Mongolia is all that is left of an empire created by Genghis Khan in the 13th century that stretched from Istanbul to Moscow and from the edge of Poland all the way to Korea! There was a time when the Mongol Empire ruled the world. The spiritual destiny of the Mongolian people has yet to be reclaimed, but it seems the Holy Spirit is raising up a new army of Mongols to invade the world—this time with the gospel!

The Mongols are egalitarian in their social structure, so the priesthood of the believers is a truth that readily finds resonance in the Mongol soul. They are a people who once ruled the world by utilizing the strength and speed of the horse, brilliant military tactics, and a ruthless will to conquer and overcome. Is this a spiritual legacy that God wants to redeem for world evangelization? Let us join our prayers with millions of other believers that the Mongol church will invade the nations—this time with a spiritual army of warriors for Christ!

## Prayer Points

- Pray for purity from sin in the newly emerging Mongolian church. Ask God to protect the leaders of the church from compromise and to know how to deal with issues of church discipline and restoration of fallen church members.
- Pray for discipleship and equipping of new believers and for their witness in the nation.
- Pray for protection from government reaction and persecution of the church.
- Pray for a missionary vision for the church so it will not become ingrown.

# Gambia

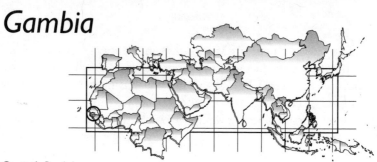

**Capital:** Banjul
**Population:** 1,100,000
**Languages:** English, Mandinka, Wolof, Fulakunda
**Major Religion:** Islam
**Major People Groups:** Mandinka, Fula, Jola, Tukuler
**Strategic Town or City:** Brikama

Founded in 1588, Gambia was Britain's first colonial posses-
sion in Africa. The 700-mile-long Gambia River enabled slave
traders to capture slaves far inland and easily transport them to
the capital, Banjul, for auction. Today, tourists are attracted to
Gambia's Atlantic beaches and lush tropical forests.

Approximately 85% of Gambia's population is Muslim, but
this was not always so. Islam first came to the West African coast
through Arab merchants and traveling teachers in the 12th century. However, it was not until the Soninke-Marabout wars in the
mid 1850s that most of the population converted to Islam. In
Gambia, as in other West African countries, Islam is mixed with
traditional animistic beliefs, witchcraft, and the worship of saints.

Gambia's political independence did not come until 1965. After a 1981 coup attempt, Senegambia, a confederation with Senegal, was formed and lasted until 1989. Gambia adopted a new constitution and held its first presidential elections in 1996.

Although largely Muslim today, Gambia maintains freedom of religion and hosts a small but growing evangelical movement. However, Christianity is often still associated with White colonialism. Missions have seen some fruit among animist peoples of the coastline, yet many Muslim communities are untouched by the gospel.

If the harsh West African coastal countries like Gambia are to be broken open for the gospel, it is going to require the sacrifice of rights, families, and yes, even lives. Such was the work of Mary Slessor, a "wild lassie" from Scotland who dedicated her life to reaching the Okoyong people (of the Okoyong River delta in what is Nigeria today). Mary went out with the Calabar Mission in 1875 and labored in simplicity, teaching, nursing, and arbitrating disputes. After her second furlough, Mary returned to Africa only to receive news that her mother had passed away. Three months later her sister died. Another sister had died while she was on furlough. Mary was alone with no attachments back home. She was overwhelmed with grief and loneliness. "There is no one to write and tell all my stories and troubles and nonsense to," she said in one letter. But press on she did. Mary accepted the death of family members as total freedom to devote herself to her new family, the African tribal people she had come to love.

In 1904, at the age of 55, Mary moved further inland along with her seven adopted children. Mary had fallen in love with a young missionary years before, but he had to return home for health reasons. Mary Slessor lived all her adult life as a single woman in Africa.

For the remaining 10 years of her life, Mary Slessor did pioneering work, leaving it to others to follow behind. Mary encountered great success with the Ibo people. In 1915, after nearly 40 years in Africa, she died at the age of 66 in her mud hut, a testimony to the selfless sacrifice of missions in the coastal jungles of West Africa. May God give us many more like Mary Slessor.

## Prayer Points

- ⤶· Thank the Lord for freedom to proclaim the gospel in Gambia. Ask the Lord to give Muslims the openness of heart to receive it.

- ⤶· Intercede for the church to direct its efforts at reaching Muslims and planting many new churches. Pray particularly for the Mandingo people of *Roots* fame.

- ⤶· Lift up the Gambian Christians, that they would develop a distinctly Gambian church that would change perceptions of Christianity as a White-man's religion.

- ⤶· Believe God for a new wave of missionaries with servant hearts and skills to come alongside the poor. Ask God to raise up a final thrust that will lead the evangelization of every person in Muslim Africa!

- ⤶· Gambia is open, so ask the Lord how to pray in cooperation with the Holy Spirit and what He wants to do today in this small but strategic African country. God hears and answers prayer!

# A Closing Prayer

Perhaps you've prayed through this book and God has been speaking to your heart. I ask you to seriously consider that He may be calling you to go, to be one of the workers you've asked Him for repeatedly during your prayer times. You obviously have a heart to see Jesus glorified in all the nations of the world. Please just don't assume that God wants you to stay where you are. Ask Him. He may have a very specific reason for keeping you where you've always been, but He also may be calling you to spread His glory to the nations.

There is a place for people from every stage of life on the mission field: a recent high school graduate or retiree, a single adult or a family with young children. I'm not saying it will be easy; in fact, Jesus promised that we will face tribulation. But I can promise you that it will be worth it. I encourage you to go back through this book prayerfully; see if there is a particular country that God lays on your heart. If you have no idea how to get there, you can contact one of the organizations on the next page or talk to your pastor, but by all means, get more information.

I'm not trying to recruit you to any particular organization or ministry, nor am I trying to put a guilt trip on you, but I believe it is a cry from the Lord of the Harvest to raise up more laborers to bring in the harvest. Please know that this manuscript has been prayed over fervently and that we have asked God to use it to challenge people to go. If your heart is stirred, perhaps even pounding inexplicably, you may be the next worker our Lord is calling. It is my prayer that God will put a divine restlessness in you if indeed you are one He desires to send into the harvest field. May you not rest until you pursue the calling He is placing on your heart!

Dear Jesus,

I lay my life before You right now to do with it anything You desire. My deepest heart's cry, Lord, is to see You glorified by people from every culture, every language, and every people group in the world. You are worthy, Jesus. I lay before You my gifts, talents, dreams, and plans and ask You to do with them what You please. I will go anywhere You send me. I trust You to give me direction and meet my needs, for You are able. Show me the way You want me to go, and build in me the desire and conviction to pursue that path with passion. And may I be a person who worships You every day by how I live my life, how I love those around me, and how I share Your light with everyone I encounter.

For Your glory, Jesus. Amen.

# Acknowledgements
# and Grateful Thanks

Thank you to Luis Bush for his invitation to write this book. It has been refreshing to my soul to renew acquaintances with 64 old friends!

And thank you to Bev Pegues at Christian Information Network. Your enthusiasm for the glory of God in the nations makes me smile while I work. Thank you, Bev. It is a privilege to partner with you.

And to Keri Weirich, who typed, researched, prayed, wept over the nations, and believed God with me for a tool to change people's lives. Bless you, Keri. God answered those prayers in Costa Rica!

And to my wife and best friend, Sally. I love you more now than when we started.

Floyd McClung
Floyds.office@USA.ORG

# Resources

 The mission of *The Christian Broadcasting Network, Inc.* and its affiliated organizations is to...

...prepare the United States of America and the nations of the world for the coming of Jesus Christ and the establishment of the Kingdom of God on earth. Our ultimate goal is to achieve a time in history when "the knowledge of the Lord will cover the earth as the waters cover the sea."

In achieving our mission our chief method is the strategic use of all forms of mass communication and the conduct of education that will train the young and old to understand how the principles of the Kingdom of God relate to those spheres of human endeavor which play a dominant role in our world.

In achieving our mission nothing should be done that does not glorify God and His son Jesus Christ.

The strategy of WorldReach, CBN's vision to reap a spiritual harvest around the world, is the development of partnerships with other Christian organizations in order to maximize resources and impact. By partnering with other ministries with world outreaches, CBN expects to minimize duplication of efforts and create a spiritual synergy that will multiply the effect of the various methodologies that will be employed by WorldReach.

In the fulfillment of our mission, as to calling and message, CBN's Biblical role model is John the Baptist. As to wisdom it is Solomon. As to ministry to Israel it is the prophet Ezekiel. In all that we are, do, and say ~ it is Jesus Christ.

...Matthew 28:19,20

# Christian Information Network

## MOBILIZING PRAYER FOR THE UNREACHED

*Colorado Springs, CO*

The mission of the Christian Information Network is to mobilize prayer for and coordinate prayer journeys into the 10/40 Window. CIN provides information and training to the Body of Christ. This is accomplished by partnering with churches, ministries, and home-based intercessors.

As never before, God is stirring the hearts of His people to prayer! The response to the *Praying Through The Window* initiatives has been overwhelming. Believers from more than 100 nations spanning many denominations and evangelical groups have united to pray for the 10/40 Window in an unprecedented way.

***Praying Through The Window II*** **- 1993, Focused on the 10/40 Window Nations** –More than 21 million Believers participated worldwide!

***Praying Through The Window II*** **- 1995, Focused on the 100 Gateway Cities of the 10/40 Window** –More than 35 million Believers worldwide stood in the gap for the lost in the 10/40 Window.

***Praying Through The Window III*** **- 1997, Focused on the Unreached People Groups of the 10/40 Window** –It has been estimated that more than 35 million Believers participated! The final results will be published by the Spring of 1999.

***Praying Through The Window IV*** **- 1999, Focuses on the 10/40 Window Nations** –Will culminate in October of 1999!

As a result of these unified efforts, amazing and documented changes are taking place in the countries of the 10/40 Window. Many exciting developments are reported in the new book, THE MOVE OF THE HOLY SPIRIT IN THE 10/40 WINDOW. The Christian Information Network offers a variety of unique resources for intercessors and those interested in missions. Please visit the resources section of our website (www.christian-info.com), or contact us at the address below.

Join millions of Believers worldwide in praying for the precious people in the 10/40 Window. Register your commitment to pray, and receive your free copy of the 1999 prayer calendar by contacting the Christian Information Network today. Unity and agreement in prayer yields astonishing results!

Christian Information Network®
11005 State Hwy 83 N ◆ Suite 159 ◆ Colorado Springs, CO 80921 USA
Tel: 1(719) 522-1040 ◆ Fax: 1(719) 277-7148 ◆ Email: cin@cin1040.net

# Global Harvest Ministries
## AD 2000 UNITED PRAYER TRACK
*Colorado Springs, CO*

Located in the World Prayer Center in Colorado Springs, Global Harvest Ministries has the following objectives:

- To catalyze and strengthen global forces for evangelization.
- To mobilize prayer for world evangelization.
- To train Christian leaders in prayer, spiritual warfare, and other aspects of practical ministry.
- To support, encourage, and facilitate the spread and growth of the Christian faith throughout the world.
- To support other organizations, projects and initiatives that are organized and operated for similar purposes.

Global Harvest Ministries
AD 2000 United Prayer Track
P.O. Box 63060, Colorado Springs, CO 80962-3060, USA
Phone 1 (719) 262 9922, FAX 1 (719) 262 9920, Email
74114.570@compuserve.com

# Campus Crusade for Christ

Campus Crusade for Christ is an interdenominational movement to help fulfill the Great Commission through discipleship and evangelism, using the multiplication strategy of "win-build-send": *winning* people to Christ, *building* them to share their faith, then *sending* them to do likewise.

Beginning in 1951, Bill and Vonette Bright launched Campus Crusade for Christ on the campus of UCLA in Los Angeles as the first step in helping to fulfill the Great commission—to help give every person on earth the opportunity to say "yes" to Jesus Christ, in every country and every culture. Forty-seven years later the ministry has grown to more than 300,000 full-time and trained volunteer staff in 172 countries. One of the 55 ministries of Campus Crusade for Christ is the "JESUS" film, a full-length movie on the life of Christ taken directly from the Gospel of Luke. This film is now in a record-breaking 472 languages and has been viewed by 1.7 billion people in 223 countries. Tens, if not hundreds of millions, have indicated salvation decisions for Christ.

Working together with millions of Christians from thousands of churches of all denominations, plus hundreds of missions groups, as of January 1, 1999 the gospel has been taken to over 3 billion people, about one-half the world's current population. More than 100,000 churches of many denominations have been established. Working with all these cooperating Christians, churches and groups, we are committed to complete the fulfillment of the Great Commission by the end of the year 2000, which is the end of this millennium.

Campus Crusade for Christ resources the churches through training in discipleship and evangelism, and with materials including more than 50 books and booklets on these subjects and others, such as fasting and prayer, holiness of life, and many related subjects.

Please pray for the necessary manpower and money to finish the task the Lord has given us.

The 55 ministries under the umbrella of Campus Crusade for Christ reach just about every segment of the population and also include:

- Campus Ministry (college)
- Church Life (lay ministry)
- Student Venture (high school)
- Military Ministry
- Athletes in Action
- Josh McDowell Ministry
- Executive Ministry
- Justice LINC (prison ministry)
- Keynote Communications (music)
- Family Life
- Seven International Schools of Theology
- Women Today
- The Great Commission Prayer Movement (prayer ministry)*
- WorldChangers Radio
- The JESUS Film Project
- Christian Embassies in many capitals of the world
- *And many more.*

*Will continue to give direction to prayers for the 10/40 Window after October 1999.

**Anyone may write or telephone for more information about any of these or other ministries. Contact: 100 Sunport Lane, Orlando, FL 32809, (407) 826-2000, *http://www.ccci.org*.**

# WANTED!

## By Campus Crusade for Christ

Christian persons who will accept
Prayer responsibility for a Frontier
Field...in a city of their choice:

- A Million People Target Area, or
- A Level One University, with
    high enrollment and prominence,
- Or a hub city—a population center
    with strong national influence.

## ARE YOU AVAILABLE?

Write or call -
Great Commission Prayer Movement
100 Sunport Lane   Dept. 2800
Orlando, Florida   32809
        Phone:  407/826-2884
        FAX     407/826-2851

# Billions Still Live in Darkness...

*YWAM Strategic Frontiers International is piercing the darkness of Islam, Hinduism, and Buddhism in the 10/40 Window with the Light of Christ... Come and Join Us!!!*

**Training Opportunities**
- Discipleship Training School (DTS) & Crossroads Discipleship Training School (CDTS) – January, April & September
- School Of Strategic Missions (SOSM) – September
- Applied Biblical Foundations (ABF) – April

**Outreach Opportunities**
- Join our Evangelism & Church Planting Teams in Azerbaijan, Morocco, Pakistan, India, The Himalayan Range, and throughout the 10/40 Window
- Mission Adventures — Summer Youth Group Outreaches
- Join our Research Expeditions & Prayer Journey Teams into the 10/40 Window.

**Local Church Mobilization**
- The Alliance — partnering to transform nations
- Mission Challenge School — Mini-DTS held in churches
- Missions-Minded music groups for Youth Services
- YWAM SF Speakers for Conferences & Seminars
- Workshop On Strategic Prayer

# Every Home for Christ
## *Touching the World with the Gospel*
### Colorado Springs, CO

The mission of Every Home for Christ is to serve the Body of Christ in equipping and mobilizing believers everywhere to pray for and actively participate in the personal presentation of a printed or repeatable message of the Gospel of Jesus Christ, systematically, to every home in the whole world, adding new believers as functioning members of the Church.

Since 1946, Every Home for Christ, with a full-time staff of 2,000 workers plus 8,000 volunteer associates, has distributed over 1.9 billion gospel booklets in 187 nations, resulting in over 25 million decision cards. EHC has also been instrumental in planting more than 36,000 New Testament home fellowships called Christ Groups, most within the 10/40 Window. Where illiterate people groups exist, EHC distributes gospel records and audiotapes, including the amazing "card talks" (cardboard record players). In a recent 12-month period 1,485,284 decision cards were received in EHC offices around the world, or an average of 4,069 every day!

Because many areas of the world are virtually closed to all missionary outreach, particularly in Muslim countries as well as the remaining Communist nations, such as China and North Korea, Every Home for Christ has developed an especially strong prayer mobilization effort through its multihour *Change the World School of Prayer* originated by Dick Eastman, EHC's International President. More than 2,000,000 Christians in 120 nations have been impacted by this substantive challenge to pray for world evangelization.

Dick Eastman is also the author of numerous best-selling books on prayer and devotional growth that have been used by God to strengthen more than 1.5 million Christians in at least 20 major languages throughout the world. Prayer resources from EHC include:

**Beyond Imagination: A Simple Plan to Save the World**—illustrates the powerful move of the Holy Spirit taking place in more than 100 countries worldwide, especially the 10/40 Window.

**The Jericho Hour**—explains barriers that still hinder world evangelization in the 10/40 Window, and offers practical advice to prayerfully confront these strongholds.

**No Easy Road: Inspirational Thoughts on Prayer**—forming and nurturing a passion for daily prayer.

**The Hour That Changes the World**—practical devotional suggestions with a unique, time-tested 12-step prayer strategy that impacts the world.

**Love On Its Knees**—principles of intercession to help pray with dramatic effectiveness for unknown people in regions like the 10/40 Window.

**Living and Praying in Jesus' Name**—a study of the names and titles of Jesus in Scripture (by Dick Eastman and Jack Hayford).

**The Change the World School of Prayer**—a multihour course that is excellent for prayer journeying teams.

**EHC's *10/40 Window Edition* World Prayer Map**—one of the best visual aids to help intercessors pray strategically for the world. Every country and its corresponding leader is identified, along with an alphabetical listing of major ministries working to spread the Gospel globally.

For additional information, or a free resource catalog, write: Every Home for Christ • P.O. Box 35930 Colorado Springs, CO 80935 • (800) 423-5054 • (719) 260-8888 • Visit EHC's website at: www.sni.net/ehc